4th Edition

Learning Disability Today

The essential guide for support staff, service providers, families and students

Edited by

Eddie Chaplin, with Marian Jennings,
Gill Concannon, Renee Francis,
Jo Delree and Lesley Bedford

Learning Disability Today, 4th Edition

The essential guide for support staff, service providers, families and students

Published by:
Pavilion Publishing and Media Ltd
Rayford House
School Road
Hove
East Sussex
BN3 5HX
Tel: 01273 434 943
Fax: 01273 227 308
Email: info@pavpub.com

Published 2018

A catalogue record for this book is available from the British Library.

ISBN: 978-1-911028-69-7

Pavilion is the leading training and development provider and publisher in the health, social care and allied fields, providing a range of innovative training solutions underpinned by sound research and professional values. We aim to put our customers first, through excellent customer service and value.

Authors: Eddie Chaplin, with Marian Jennings, Gill Concannon, Renee Francis, Jo Delree and Lesley Bedford
Production editor: Mike Benge, Pavilion Publishing and Media Ltd
Cover design: Phil Morash, Pavilion Publishing and Media Ltd
Page layout and typesetting: Emma Dawe, Pavilion Publishing and Media Ltd
Printing: CMP Digital Print Solutions

Contents

About the contributors

The *Can You Understand It?* team

Jessica Burman works for Oxleas NHS Foundation Trust as a speech and language therapy specialist support worker in an Adult Learning Disability and Mental Health inpatient unit. She is also a member of the *Can You Understand it?* team. Jessica assists the speech and language therapist to assess service users' communication and develop interventions to maximise their understanding and their ability to express themselves. Jessica supports the inpatient service to provide information to service users that is accessible and helps them to create an 'Inclusive Communication' environment.

Sarah Casey has been part of the *Can you understand it?* team for the last three years and is also part of the 'Respect' group for Bexley Mencap. Sarah has helped with learning disability presentations and taken part in a video about hospital passports. Sarah enjoys taking part in swimming competitions as well as teaching people with learning disabilities to swim.

John Clarke is one of the founder members of the *Can you understand it?* team, established eight years ago. John has been an assistant MP for Health for the People's Parliament in Greenwich, a health quality checker and an employment ambassador ensuring that people with learning disabilities who are in employment are treated fairly. John has lots of experience being on interview panels and has given presentations to governors and managers in Oxleas. John loves art and music.

Dennis Hayward joined the *Can you understand it?* team four years ago. He enjoys coming to the team meetings and finds it interesting being part of the team. He has been part of Oxleas' service user interview panel and taken part in a video about hospital passports. Dennis likes arts and crafts, reading, music (60s & 80s), going shopping and holidays.

Steve Hardy is practice development nurse in the Adult Learning Disability Service of Oxleas NHS Foundation Trust and a member of the *Can You Understand It?* team. He is also associate editor of the *Advances in Autism* journal and a member of LDNurse.com. He is well published in the field of the mental health needs of people with learning disabilities and mental capacity. He has a passion for developing and sharing resources and work in co-production with people with learning disabilities to give them a platform to be heard.

James Holmes has been part of the *Can you understand it?* team for the last five years. He has taken part in a number of projects like looking at signage in hospitals and being part of the Oxleas' interview panel. He has also been learning support assistant at college, helping people with learning disabilities to use computers. He enjoys playing tennis and football, going out and gardening.

Sarah Leatherdale joined the team three years ago and has also been on the service user interview panel for Oxleas. Sarah is also part of the 'Respect' group for Bexley Mencap and has taken part in videos about hospital passports. Sarah enjoys going out.

Sharon Rodrigues is the patient information lead for Oxleas' Learning Disability Directorate. Her main role is facilitating the *Can you understand it?* team, ensuring information for people with learning disabilities is accessible and provides Easy Read training for staff. She previously worked in an in-patient unit for people with learning disabilities focusing on person centred approaches and being a voice for the patients. She has recently also been part of the Accessible Information Standard Working party ensuring the standard is being implemented in the trust.

Chris Saxton has enjoyed being part of the team for two years. Chris attends Astley Day Centre and also has a job cleaning windows supported by Mencap. Chris enjoys going to football matches and supports Arsenal.

Sunny Sokhal has been part of the team for seven years and has taken part in a number of learning disability events, been part of service user interview panels and looked at signage round hospitals. Sunny is part of the 'Speaking up' group for Advocacy for All and is very committed to ensuring people with learning disabilities have a voice. Sunny enjoys playing football and going to the cinema.

Paula Abreu is a highly specialist speech and language therapist who graduated with a BSC (Hons) in Speech and Language Pathology and Therapeutics in 1990. Following on from this she has gained an M.Ed. in Speech and Language Difficulties and has over 25 years' experience in a range of clinical and educational settings, working as a practitioner with children and young people with communication difficulties and their families. In addition to her clinical work, Paula is committed to increasing knowledge of communication needs in developing professionals and has links with several tertiary educational establishments, including London South Bank University where she is a regular guest lecturer in the School of Health and Social Care.

Barbara Barter is consultant clinical psychologist working with the Mental Health in Learning Disabilities team at the South London and Maudsely NHS Trust (SLaM) and is a clinical tutor with the IoPPN DClin Psych training programme at King's College London. Barbara has worked with individuals with learning disabilities before and since qualifying as a clinical psychologist at the University of Wales, Bangor, in 2010. She has an interest in behavioural and third wave approaches to supporting individuals with LD and their networks.

Kieron Beard is a senior clinical psychologist and has worked in the Mental Health in Learning Disabilities team in SLaM since qualifying from the University of Liverpool in 2013. Before undertaking his doctoral programme in clinical psychology, Dr Beard worked as a senior support worker and home manager for a specialist learning disability, challenging behaviour and intensive support service. Kieron has a special interest in human rights and social justice approaches to psychological care, enabling compassionate support networks and relational approaches to understanding mental health and distress.

Lesley Bedford is a senior lecturer in learning disability nursing at London South Bank University. Before this she was a senior lecturer on a joint programme, Learning Disability Nursing and Social Work. She is particularly keen to promote interprofessional working and teaches modules across the course. She gained her qualification in social work over 30 years ago and maintains her registration. Previous employment includes managing a local authority day centre for adults with intellectual disabilities.

Mark Brown is an independent special needs advisor and CEO of Special Help 4 Special Needs. He has worked with people with intellectual and developmental disabilities for over 30 years within a range of settings, including within residential homes and community settings. Mark has also worked with men with intellectual and developmental disabilities who have displayed inappropriate sexualised behaviour, using the SOTSEC-ID framework. Mark's work currently focuses on helping individuals of all ages with additional needs, such as autistic spectrum disorder (ASD) and intellectual and developmental disabilities, as well as those who support them, regarding a range of issues, particularly those relating to puberty, sexuality and the display of inappropriate sexualised behaviour. Since 2014, Mark has been doing a PhD at the Tizard Centre, University of Kent, focusing upon the effectiveness of the national curriculum-based sex and relationships programme (SRE) for children and young adults with ASD. Central to the research, Mark has interviewed school staff in regards to their perception of such programmes, as well as leading focus groups involving students with ASD talking about their experiences. The results and issues raised have led to the implementation of a pilot SRE programme for individuals with ASD.

Eddie Chaplin is a professor in the Department of Mental Health and Learning Disabilities at London South Bank University. Eddie has extensive clinical experience in local and national mental health services for people with neurodevelopmental disabilities, including autism, intellectual disabilities and ADHD. He has also developed a number of Masters courses relating to offending and the mental health of people with intellectual disability. Eddie has an extensive publication portfolio and is principal editor for the *Advances in Autism* journal.

Gill Concannon is a senior lecturer in learning disability nursing in the School of Health and Social Care at London South Bank University. She has over 30 years' clinical experience in a range of nursing, learning disability services and community settings. Throughout her career she has advocated lifelong learning. Since becoming a registered nurse in learning disabilities she has achieved her BSc in professional practice and MSc in clinical studies.

Peter Cronin is an expert by experience and is the elected MP for employment at the Lewisham People's Parliament. He is also a member of The Tuesday Group, for which he has spoken at a number of conferences and taken part in several national consultation exercises to raise awareness about learning disabilities.

Jo Delrée is a registered nurse for people with learning disabilities (RNLD) and a senior lecturer at London South Bank University. She has a special interest in autism spectrum conditions and people whose behaviour can be challenging to services.

Thomas Doukas is the head of inclusive research and involvement at Choice Support. His role is key for the development of inclusive research and involvement aiming to improve the lifestyles and citizenship for the people with disabilities by influencing policy and strategy. Thomas has worked with people with learning disabilities for over 14 years, focusing on research, active involvement and communication systems to ensure people with disabilities are involved in all aspects of the service provision and lead independent and fulfilling lives. Thomas's other work includes supporting people to develop accessible information, implement the Reach Standards across the organisation, set up local and regional forums, design the annual satisfaction survey, develop participation strategies for people with disabilities and their families and friends, source partnerships with external organisations, and implement the Health and Wellbeing strategy, among others.

Renée Francis is a senior lecturer in learning disability nursing at London South Bank University. Her special interests are palliative care of people with intellectual disabilities, participatory research with people with intellectual disabilities and supporting families of people with intellectual disabilities. She is also interested in interprofessional learning and ensuring key messages about the health of people with intellectual disabilities are delivered across the nursing and midwifery curriculum. Renée has been a registered learning disability nurse since 1997. In her clinical practice, Renée worked in residential services, a day service and an integrated Community Learning Disability Team. Renée was also seconded to a research project funded by the Department of Health that evaluated the use of a hand-held health record by people with intellectual disabilities. In this role, she supported a service user with intellectual disabilities to interview other service users about their health

Sally Hardy promotes a co-production approach to evaluation through action orientated innovation. She works alongside individuals, teams and organisations to promote practice driven innovations that include wide stakeholder engagement to achieve enhanced workplace cultures of effectiveness. Sally leads a team of academics at LSBU working with external health and social care partners to produce the next generation of leaders for a contemporary workforce. Her interests include psychodynamics of change as a process towards human flourishing. She leads a small team of researchers working with under served communities to influence policy change. She is currently exploring the impact and outcomes of creative arts on well-being for enhanced critical creative approaches to intergenerational mental well-being.

Marian Jennings qualified as an RNLD nurse. Marian's background is in working with people with complex disabilities. She has managed both residential and community services for adults with learning disabilities and also has extensive experience of working with people who have acquired brain injury.

Christine-Koulla Burke, Head Foundation for People with Learning Disabilities and Inequalities. Christine heads up the Mental Health Foundation's work in England on prevention and combating inequalities, as well as the Foundation for People with Learning Disabilities. She joined the Mental Health Foundation from the Institute of Applied Health and Social Policy at King's College London. Previously she worked as Deputy Chief Executive of Circles Network and as a senior manager in various organisations for over 35 years. She has developed and managed many service improvement programmes in both health and social care, and supported them to change to inclusive, person-centred services for people with learning disabilities, nationally and internationally. Christine has promoted co-production and the involvement of self-advocates and families in all programmes, and she has worked internationally on deinstitutionalisation. She supported the work of Valuing People with family leadership and managed the National Advisory Group for People with Learning Disabilities and Ethnicity. Christine has published many articles, guides and other publications, and she holds a BA Hons in Psychology, MSc in Child Psychology and a Diploma in Psychotherapy.

Andy Mantell qualified in social work at the University of Edinburgh in 1991. He specialised in hospital social work with people with neurodisability and people with mental health problems. He gained his doctorate from the University of Sussex in 2006, entitled *Huntington's Disease: The carer's story*. Since then he has been involved in training social workers at the University of Chichester and since 2015 he has been teaching nurses LSBU. He has particular interest in safeguarding adults, mental capacity, mental health and carers.

Karina Marshall-Tate is head of education and training for the Estia Centre, South London and Maudsley NHS Foundation Trust, and senior lecturer and researcher at London South Bank University. She is a learning disability nurse who has led and managed national specialist services for people with a learning disability and additional mental illness and neurodevelopmental disorders (autism/ADHD). Karina's specialist interests are in meeting the mental health needs of people with a learning disability and education and training to enhance health and social care practice and reduce health inequalities.

Annie Parris is a senior behaviour support practitioner working in the Mental Health in Learning Disabilities Team at South London & Maudsley NHS Trust. Annie has worked with individuals with learning disabilities whose behaviour is described as challenging for many years, completing a postgraduate diploma in applied psychology in learning disabilities (challenging behaviour) at the Tizard Centre, University of Kent, in 2004. She has also worked as a senior training officer at the Estia Centre and continues to be involved in updating and delivering training.

Liam Peyton is a member of the Lewisham Speaking Up group and The Tuesday Group. As a member, he has spoken at a number of conferences and taken part in several national consultations exercises to raise awareness of learning disabilities. Liam has several interests and hobbies which include college…

Peter Warburton, RNLD, RMN, Psychology BSc (Hons), is a registered nurse for people with a learning disability and also has a nursing registration in mental health. Currently he specialises in adult safeguarding and he has worked for the past five years as the safeguarding adults lead across two South London Clinical Commissioning Groups. He is a qualified best interest assessor (BIA). He has previously worked as a senior lecturer in learning disability nursing at London South Bank University. Peter has had a broad range of experience working in the public and voluntary sectors and has held local, regional and national roles. Some of his work experience is in patient safety, community nursing, health improvement, mental health and behaviour that challenges. Peter's special interest is in mental health for people who have a diagnosis on the autistic spectrum.

Peter Woodward is senior lecturer in learning disabilities at the University of Greenwich. He is a learning disabilities nurse and has worked in forensic, mental health, challenging behaviour and health services for people with learning disabilities before entering into training and then higher education.

Foreword

When choosing a book that will provide a contemporary understanding of the evidence base on a subject and yet still have a practical application in the real world, it is often the authors themselves that first attract my attention. What experience does the author have in the field? Is the writer someone who knows and understands about the 'knowledge-practice gap'? Can the author capture the essence of what nurses contribute to a person's experience of health and social care services? Well, look no further.

This latest edition of *Learning Disability Today* has been produced by an interesting collection of authors, all with a keen interest in the subject that really comes across on the page. People living with a learning disability are integrated into chapters with those who have worked across learning disability services, whether as nurses, social workers, managers or leaders, and who are now educating the next generation of health and social care providers. The breadth of experience of the authorship spans 10-40 years of working within and across health and social care settings, and this range is coupled with a pragmatism that ensures each of the chapters remains grounded in real life case examples; covering everything from the use of scented candles through to candid conversations about sexual consent. Each chapter also provides evidence that compares contemporary knowledge with political context to produce thought-provoking chapters.

A recent book written by young man with autism using an adapted keyboard has exploded the general consensus that those who cannot communicate verbally and communicate using other methods must be 'intellectually disabled'. *The Reason I Jump* by Naoki Higashida (2013) is an eloquent and captivating insight into the internal struggles of a young lad with autism. In its pages he tries desperately to fit the messy, uncomfortable cognitive process of thinking with the painfully raw emotive responses that his highly attuned internal mechanisms undergo that just don't match what's happening on the outside and therefore how others see and respond to him. He says, *'It's as if remote controlling a faulty robot; please don't judge just from the outside'* (pp 39-40).

For many years there has been limited attention paid to people living with a learning disability. The changes to the welfare systems and a persistent, significant reduction in financial support has led to a radical response to how people living with an intellectual disability are having to engage with modern society. For the first time that I can remember, we have a highly successful and internationally popular television series, Game of Thrones, that has a central character who challenges conventional 'hero' status. The inclusion of a different type of central character has brought with it an alternative feel to the programme that has allowed for convention to be pushed forward, maybe just a notch. Well, I hope this book, despite its socially challenging content, can and will challenge convention to bring a contemporary twist to a conventional text book that too will challenge how we engage with people living with a learning disability.

Sally Hardy
Professor of Mental Health and Practice Innovation
Head of Department: Mental Health and Learning Disabilities, London South Bank University

Introduction

By Peter Cronin and Liam Peyton

It is a pleasure to be asked to introduce this book and share parts of our story
that will hopefully give readers an insight into our experiences of living with
a learning disability. It is nice that the editors put the real experts first before
letting others talk about some of the things that affect people with learning
disabilities and ways to offer support and understand the issues facing people.

We are both lifelong friends and went to school together. Where we live there is
a strong learning disability community and there are many organisations such
as the Speaking Up Group, the People's Parliament, MENCAP, the Tuesday
Group, the Gateway Club and some of the local colleges and employers, who offer
opportunities to people with a learning disability. These organisations not only
support us in everyday living, but a number of them help us to raise awareness of
learning disability to others, from the general public to healthcare and education
services such as colleges and schools.

However, many people are often living without the support they need. This can be
because of a lack of services or because services do not understand what support
is required by people. This often happens to us because there are things that we
are good at, which makes people assume we are good at everything and so we can
be left in situations we find uncomfortable and where we need support but don't
have it. So, for example, someone might leave complicated forms for us to fill out
or expect us to be able to read, or they will not make information or instructions
easy for us to understand. Together, as friends, we often support each other or
other people we trust. Trust is very important – it makes a person feel secure and
confident. Often the people who support us in our housing will move on, which
makes it difficult to get to know them and to form relationships, and we then have
to get to know new people. And this is upsetting as, for those we do get to trust,
them leaving is like losing a friend.

We have written articles before about our experiences, but this book is important
to us as we have been to the LD Today conference regularly over the last few years.
Last year we not only went, but with other members of the Tuesday Group – Steve
Hardy, Eddie Chaplin and Christine Burke – we were asked to talk about our
experiences of mental health and what people can do to help them stay well. Going
to the conference and giving a talk is good as we are able to meet other people with

learning disabilities, their families and friends, as well as staff who support them. Sharing our experiences lets people learn about new things, such as mental health, and to think about how they might help themselves or support others.

Good mental health starts with feeling good about yourself. It means having the opportunities to do things that others take for granted. A good example is getting a job. We believe that, just as for everyone else, it's important for people with learning disabilities to have a job. However this can be difficult. A lot of people with learning disabilities we know really want to work but they need extra support. Sometimes this might be employers making reasonable adjustments, other times it might involve needing support to look for a job and help with application forms and interviews. Getting employment is important for people with learning disabilities as it helps us feel the same as others, and not as people who are thought to be unable to do things.

Having a job is important because:

- we are the same as other people

- we have dreams of a better future, like everyone else

- we deserve to be treated equally, but we need people to give us extra support to get treated equally

- working improves self-esteem

- working builds your confidence

- we want to be counted as part of society, doing our bit.

Getting the right support is important. We were supported by Pathways, and they can support you too, by:

- helping to do a 'job match' to see what is available and what suits your skills

- helping you to write about what you can do well and what skills you have

- helping you to put a story together about you and practise telling it to other people like you would in an interview

- support you to prepare for interviews using role-played interviews to help understand what will happen in the interview

- telling you what the person who is interviewing you is looking for

Another place that can help is the local job centre. It is good to visit with someone you know until you feel confident, as in some job centres the people working there do not know much about people with learning disabilities and this can make it difficult and stressful – you can feel rushed and it can put you off answering questions, even if you have time as it can be difficult to get out what you want to say. The person supporting you should make sure they slow down when this happens and also ask if there is information for people with learning disabilities that they can read later.

Liam's story

I've got a cleaning job in Deptford. I work two hours every Saturday. Someone from the Aurora, who provides my home, helped me to look in the paper for jobs. I saw a job I liked and thought I could do it so we filled an application form. I then got an interview. I got support at the interview. They asked me a few questions like, 'What are you like at timekeeping?' and, 'why do you want this job?'.

I got the job!

They support me every week to do the job. They show me things for the first time and then I can do it. Having a job makes me feel good about myself. I get paid monthly and it goes into my bank account.

Peter's story

My mum always thought of me. She helped me to get jobs and feel more confident. She made me feel good, always telling me I am the same as everyone else.

Pathways supported me to get a job at the Co-Op supermarket. I got a 'job coach' from Pathways. I was really nervous before, I wouldn't say boo to a goose, but they gave me confidence and understood me, and they went at my speed.

I learnt how to read bar codes, put fresh food at the back and older food at the front. I stack shelves, take out-of-date food, I wrap up the cages with boxes so they won't blow anywhere. I really enjoy helping other people – they call this customer service. If someone can't find what they are looking for, like cereal, I take them to the right aisle.

I work there every Tuesday from 10am to 2pm and I get paid every month, which goes straight into bank account. And I spend the money down the pub... No, I'm joking! I'm saving up my wages to go on holiday to Southend. My friends are really proud of me and I'm really proud of them. I'm still looking for another job, like caring for older people.

We enjoy our jobs but we sometimes feel we don't get the same chances as others. Our jobs are only for a few hours a week and this is the same for many people with learning disabilities. Most of us would like to do more or increase our hours, but in a lot of places there is little opportunity to do this. This seems unfair, particularly when we see other people without learning disabilities get more work or get promoted. It is important, whatever job a person has, for staff to support and encourage them by explaining things clearly in a way the person understands, and to have patience while they learn.

Often, people supporting us will just see it as their job to give help. For us to be included, support staff need to think about what we might be missing and support us to do other things that are taken for granted. Although we are in our 40s, until the last general election neither of us had voted as no one had ever supported us to be on the electoral register. It is important for everyone to have the right to vote and stand up for their rights. Previously, I (Peter) asked my outreach worker if I can be registered to vote and he just said, 'Don't worry about it now, we'll do it later'. I never got registered. Not being able to do these things does affect your self-esteem as you think people feel they are better than you and treat you like a child rather than an adult.

Not everyone is like this though. We had a visit from MENCAP before the last election who were so supportive, giving us advice so we could make up our own minds about who to vote for. Eventually, although I never got any help from my Outreach, Steve from the Tuesday Group helped me to register and supported me to vote. To help understand the ballot paper we had sessions on the symbols and colours of each of the parties. When we got there, though, we were able to tell the staff that I needed support because of my learning disability.

Having a job and voting are both things that make us feel that people are treating us the same as everyone else, and that we are doing things for others and having a say. Both of these are good for our mental health, which we started talking about at the beginning of this chapter. To finish, we want to share some more about good mental health and the things that can get in the way, which we told people at the LD Today conference in 2016.

Not everyone who has mental health problems experiences the same things. Poor mental health might affect your sleep, appetite and enjoyment. This can be made worse if those supporting you don't know about mental health. For some people with learning disabilities, it can be hard to describe their feelings. People with learning disabilities are more at risk of mental health problems for many reasons and are more likely to:

- have little money

- have other people telling them what to do and making decisions for them

- have few friends or opportunities to do activities that others enjoy

- suffer from long-term health problems and disabilities

- suffer from physical problems due to self-neglect e.g. poor dental hygiene or diet

- have fewer people who can support them

- experience abuse from others in the community, such as school children

- pestering for money

- struggle to find work or go to college

- experience problems when trusted support staff leave, which makes us upset

- have support workers who tell us to wait and talk to the next shift.

(Cronin *et al*, 2017)

When people with learning disabilities go to get help for mental health problems, it can often be a bad experience. Here are some of the experiences that we have had or that people have told us about:

- The people who support them do not know them or what they have been going through.

- The doctor or receptionist will ignore the person with learning disabilities and will talk only to the person supporting them.

- One person was shouted at for not going to see the doctor when his name came up on the screen. The receptionist did not know he could not read.

- Sometimes it is difficult to understand what the doctor is asking the person or remember how long things have been going on.

- Some people feel they are not listened to or are rushed and that the doctor doesn't understand about their learning disabilities.

It is important to get help as soon as you feel there is a problem and to do things to help stop problems happening. It is also important to have good coping strategies, such as breathing exercises or hobbies, and to write a plan about staying healthy. Everyone is different, so what works for one person will not work for another. Looking after our mental health is as important as looking after our physical health. From our experience of talking to other people with learning disabilities, the following things can be helpful:

- Speak to someone you can trust, such as family or key worker. If no one is around then some people find the Samaritans good to talk to as they are good at listening to problems.

- Go to the GP for regular health check ups.

- Keep active, doing exercise or going out to do something you enjoy.

- Relax and have time to yourself, such as watching TV or listening to music.

- Make sure you look after yourself and try not to let things pile up, such as cleaning or having to go shopping.

- Have a hobby or interest, such as doing exercise, collecting things or visiting museums. These things are very good at helping to avoid boredom.

Most of know the things that make us feel stressed. It is good to tell people and get support around how to manage stressful situations. For example, we practice at the Tuesday Group how to say 'no' to strangers who ask for money. Even practising is hard when you know the person but it can make it easier when you go out and it happens in real life. This is difficult in real life, and if you feel nervous or in danger then it is better to try and avoid the situation. You can go a different way or cross over the road at a different place so you don't see them.

Final thoughts

We would like to thank Pavilion Publishing for letting us write this chapter, and to Eddie Chaplin and Steve Hardy who supported us to put it together. If you see us at conferences, do come and say hello – the more people who are aware of learning disabilities the better our lives will be. We hope to make people think and to realise that sometimes they can hurt people with learning disabilities even when they don't mean to by saying things without thinking. We don't mean people saying rude things, or using horrible, old-fashioned words to describe us, but many people don't even realise what they're saying, such as, 'Don't be daft' or, 'Why are you taking so long to do such a simple thing?'

References

Cronin *et al*, 2017

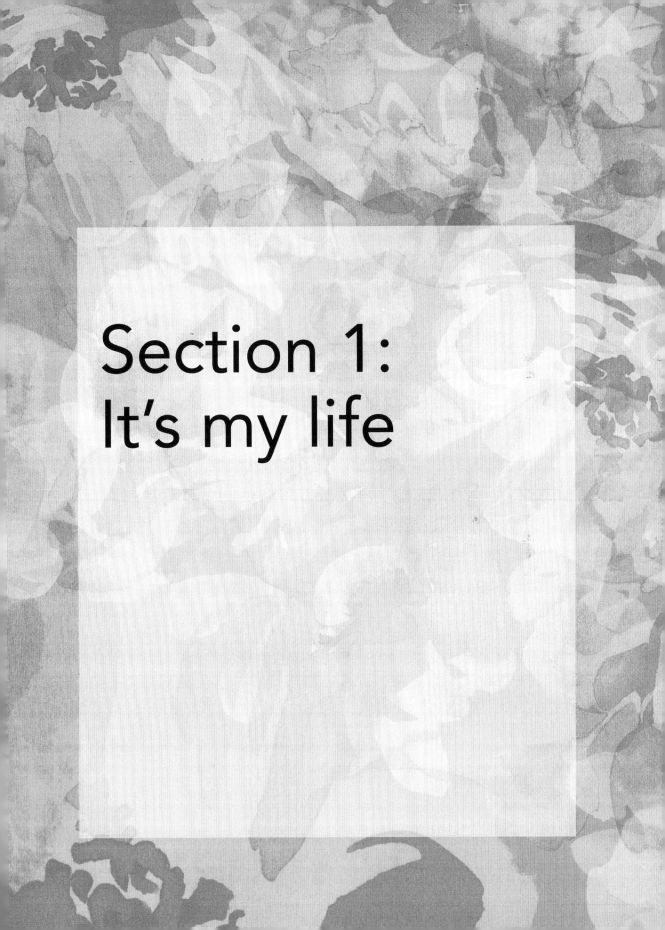

Section 1:
It's my life

Chapter 1:

What does having a learning disability mean to us?

By Members of the Can you Understand it? team at Oxleas NHS Foundation: Jessica Burman, Sarah Casey, John Clarke, Dennis Hayward, Steve Hardy, James Holmes, Sarah Leatherdale, Sharon Rodrigues, Chris Saxton, Sunny Sokhal

Aims and summary

The aims of this chapter are to share our experiences of having a learning disability and what it means to us in everyday life

In this chapter, we in the *Can You Understand It?* team reflect on what having a learning disability means to us. We also discuss some of our experiences from when we were younger, and we finish the chapter with positive experiences and our achievements.

What does having a learning disability mean to us?

Learning disability means that people need to get to know you inside and out. We may have difficulties with communication and we may need extra time when learning something. If we have problems, sometimes we may need support to come up with an answer. But please remember that we have feelings and emotions, and that we have learning disabilities – we think this is called 'living experience'! Please think about words you use, as we might get upset. Here are some examples of experiences from members of the team:

'I used to get called handicapped or retard. It made me feel like rubbish, that I'm not as good as them.'

'Most of the time its school kids calling you names, like spastic, mong or weirdo. But sometimes its adults that call us names. This really hurts.'

'Yes adults should know better, picking on people with learning disabilities, it's not fair.'

Having an IQ test and what does it mean?

We had to look up what IQ means – it stands for Intelligence Quotient. We understand what intelligence means but we are not sure about quotient! Most of us in the *Can You Understand It?* team have had IQ tests but these happened when we were at school. An IQ test assesses your general knowledge, you have to do puzzles and describe what words mean. But some of us were at a disadvantage because we couldn't read or write. It really helps if you know the person who is testing you; it makes you feel at ease.

Communication

Communication is so important to people with learning disabilities and those who support them. It is especially important to the *Can You Understand It?* team because we are an editorial team who review how good Easy Read is and make recommendations. Being able to understand others is vital, as is them being able understand you. Good communication is key to supporting people with learning disabilities.

'At school I had a speech therapist – they taught me how to speak, and use words clearly. They showed me how to use a tape recorder to help my communication. I used it to play back what I just heard and then I repeat it back. This really helped me.'

Reading and writing

Reading and writing can be difficult for anyone to learn, but when you add in learning disabilities it becomes even harder. Sometimes people with learning disabilities don't like telling people they have trouble reading. You sometimes pretend like you have understood what is read or has been said. But it really helps you if you tell the person that you need support. There is no shame in having a learning disability.

'I had to stay in after school for extra classes, this helped me. I looked at it as I was getting an education. I didn't mind it but it just took a bit longer.'

'I had problems reading small print and I had to get someone to sit down and help me. Also, at the meetings they print out everything in big writing for me.'

'When I was a child I had problems with reading and writing and, because of my hearing problem, it made it hard. I was a bit nervous but I had to admit I had a learning disability.'

'It took me ages to read and write and some people were faster at learning, they could read better than me. I found it a bit worrying.'

Telling the time

Everyone learns to tell the time when they are a child, but having a learning disability makes it a bit harder. Telling the time seems such a simple thing to do but it causes problems if you have problems reading a clock. You need to read the time, especially if you live by yourself. You need to need know what time to get up, if you have a GP appointment or are going to work or college. Often it makes you late.

'I used to make mistakes. Like, I used to say, 'It's a quarter past fifteen or half-past twenty. Then I got a talking clock at home, like clocks for the blind. This really changed my life and it's so easy to use a talking clock.'

'It took me longer to tell the time but I can tell the time now. They taught me with a large clock and asked me to do paperwork. I had to write down what time it is next to the clock.'

Travelling

Travelling alone helps you become independent. But to do this you need lots of skills. You need to be able to read a map or directions. You might need to know which way is north or south, how long a mile is and where you get the 422 bus from. It is so complex and confusing. Things that might help are Easy Read signs, talking maps and using basic symbols.

'I hate getting on buses during rush hour because of the noise and swearing – it's not on.'

'I have problems telling timetables for trains, like when it says it's delayed and then the pre-recording. You need to ask for help on trains and at the station but sometimes it's embarrassing.'

'People with autism might find travelling hard, especially in crowds or lots of noise.'

Using money

Being able to use money helps you in everyday life. It's great if you have support workers or family. But what if you only get a few hours of outreach support a week or don't get any support? You need to be good at maths and recognise the difference between notes and coins. Most people use computers to pay bills but many people with learning disabilities don't have enough money for a computer or know how to use one. So we have to pay at the post office or bank, which means standing in queues and hoping the person is kind and understands what having a learning disability is like.

'I still don't know about money so my support workers manage the money for me. I'm used to it now.'

'People standing behind in shopping queues sometimes get annoyed or have a go at you. Can't they just wait a little bit longer? Everyone needs help sometimes.'

'I show people a card that says I have a learning disability and will need extra time.'

'My maths wasn't good at school; I know how to add up but I can't do hard things like percentages. I did much better at science and one day I made a volcano. And in woodwork I made a guitar.'

Looking on the positive side

It's so easy to only think about the negative side of things, but everyone should always take time to look at their achievements, no matter how small. All of us at the *Can You Understand It?* team have made loads of achievements and we are all proud of what we have done. Like writing this chapter is good for our self-esteem. We all take part in interviewing staff, like nurses, psychiatrists and occupational therapists. We rate them on how they answer questions but also on how smartly they are dressed, their body language, making eye contact, and, most importantly, 'don't use jargon'!

One of us had a job as a 'quality checker'. This means going into GP surgeries and checking things like signs, Easy Read information, how the receptionist acts and how easy it is to understand the doctor. We also speak to patients with learning disabilities and it's really important that they speak to the patient first and not the carers. Being a 'quality checker' makes you feel so good and happy.

One of us recently wrote a blog for LearningDisabilityNurse.com. The blog told the true story of how people with learning disabilities can help in an emergency. All of us have been on the cover of Oxleas (NHS Foundation Trust) magazine and we have made videos about health and hospital passports.

Conclusion

We are so proud of being members of the *Can You Understand It?* team and all of us have come on in leaps and bounds. We support each other and look forward to the future. We are people first, and if you look past the disability you might see a person.

Key learning points

These is what we hope you have learned about us:

- Growing up with a learning disability can be more difficult without support.

- Be patient with us – if we don't get it at first or are slow carrying out tasks, please don't be rude.

- There are many ways to learn and achieve things so we can join in, such as Easy Read, talking or digital clocks.

- Despite this there is lots we can do and our group helps us let people understand about learning disabilities and some of our achievements, like writing this chapter.

Chapter 2:

Positive Behavioural Support – enhancing quality of life for people with learning disabilities whose behaviour is considered challenging

By Barbara Barter, Annie Parris and Kieron Beard

Aims

The aims of this chapter are to:

- introduce what is meant by term 'behaviour that challenges'
- discuss key behavioural theory
- outline a model to understand behaviour that challenges
- introduce Positive Behavioural Support and outline the core components of this approach, including its emphasis on reducing restrictive practices
- describe a case example using Positive Behavioural Support.

Summary

Challenging behaviour is generally thought of as behaviour that causes difficulty or harm to a person or to the people around them. Often, the response from others is to try and stop that person from engaging in the behaviour to ensure their safety and the safety of others. The main problem, however, is that this often means restricting someone's choices, such as limiting their access to the community. These restrictive interventions can therefore limit that person's quality of life.

When supporting someone whose behaviour is described as challenging, the 'challenge' is to find a way to support that individual to achieve the best quality of life while also supporting them, and others, to stay safe and well.
In this chapter, we discuss an approach to challenging behaviour that aims to

achieve just that, called Positive Behavioural Support (PBS). We describe our understanding of challenging behaviour and outline PBS as an approach to supporting individuals to live meaningful lives while maintaining well-being.

What is behaviour that challenges?

Emerson (2001) defined challenging behaviour as:

'...culturally abnormal behaviour(s) of such an intensity, frequency or duration that the physical safety of the person or others is likely to be placed in serious jeopardy, or behaviour which is likely to seriously limit use of, or result in the person being denied access to, ordinary community facilities.'

This term can include a large range of behaviours, from rocking, shouting, swearing or spitting, up to physical aggression, self-injurious behaviours or behaviour that is destructive to property. Behaviour that challenges is not a diagnosis or a mental health difficulty, and it can vary in terms of presence and impact in differing environments. For example, what may seem 'challenging' in a classroom setting may not be considered challenging at home.

How common is it?

It is understood that around 5–15% of individuals with a learning disability in educational, health or social care services develop behaviour that challenges, and it is more common for people with severe disability. Rates are higher in teenagers and people in their early 20s, as well as in particular settings such hospitals, where rates are as high as 30–40%. People with a learning disability who also have communication difficulties, autism, sensory impairments, sensory processing difficulties and physical or mental health problems, including dementia, may be more likely to develop behaviour that challenges (NICE, 2015).

Theory of learnt behaviour

Behaviour is understood as functional – that is, behaviour happens for a reason. We call the process whereby someone learns a particular behaviour as 'operant conditioning'. That is, behaviour is learned through the consequences of that particular behaviour. People may often describe what happens before a behaviour (e.g. someone was shouting because they were frustrated), however the important aspect that is often missed is what happens as a result of someone's behaviour (e.g. the person was no longer asked to do something after they had shouted).

As psychologists and behaviour support practitioners, we are interested in understanding the consequences of behaviour in order to understand how we can support that individual to achieve the same outcome without having to engage in behaviour that challenges.

For example, Paul lives in a busy supported living accommodation with five other residents. He doesn't enjoy taking part in household tasks, and whenever he is asked to wash the dishes he bangs his head with his fist. Staff then stop asking him to wash up.

Antecedent	Behaviour	Consequence
→	→	
Asked to wash up	Banging head with fist	Remove request

We call this the process of reinforcement. In this example, the behaviour of heading banging is reinforced because Paul has learned that this behaviour is effective in reducing demands upon him and it is very likely that he will use this behaviour again.

Research says that the four main consequences of behaviour are:

- Access to tangibles: 'I want that!'
- Access to interaction: 'Talk to me/spend time with me!'
- Sensory stimulation: 'That feels nice.'
- Escape from interaction/demand: 'I don't want to do that!'

Common causes of behaviour that challenges

There are both internal and environmental causes of behaviour that challenges. Examples of internal factors include being in pain, being unwell, being tired, the effects of medication, physical health difficulties, sensory difficulties and, very importantly and commonly, communication difficulties – both understanding and expressing needs. Some specific genetic syndromes are also commonly associated with particular behavioural difficulties, such as Prader Willi syndrome, which is often associated with behavioural difficulties around food.

Examples of environmental factors include noise, boredom, lighting, temperature, quality of interaction and access to meaningful activities, and many others.

A model to understand behaviour that challenges

These two elements taken together, the internal and environmental/external, can help us understand a general model of behaviour that challenges, as outlined in Figure 1.1. Individuals with LD may have particular biological (internal) or psychosocial (external) factors influencing their behaviour, as shown under 'Vulnerabilities' on the left of the diagram. 'Maintaining processes', in the centre, are the particular consequences of that behaviour which serve to reinforce that behaviour, or make it more likely to happen again. On the right of the diagram, the impact of challenging behaviour is social; that is, it can lead to harm to the self or to others, or it can lead to exclusion. This in turn can feed back into the person's psychosocial vulnerability to challenging behaviour.

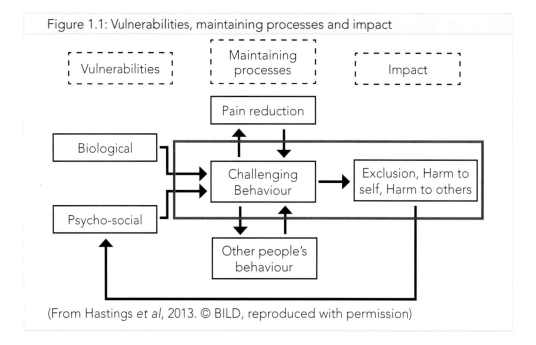

Figure 1.1: Vulnerabilities, maintaining processes and impact

(From Hastings *et al*, 2013. © BILD, reproduced with permission)

What is Positive Behavioural Support?

PBS is a framework for developing an understanding of behaviour that challenges, rather than a single therapeutic approach or intervention. It is based on the assessment of the social and physical context – that is, the internal and external factors – in which the behaviour occurs. By understanding all of the factors that possibly contribute to a particular behaviour, interventions are designed that enhance quality of life outcomes for both the person themselves and their carers or support worker (Gore *et al*, 2013). BILD have produced a helpful video that gives an overview of PBS: www.bild.org.uk/capbs/pbsinformation/introduction-to-pbs/.

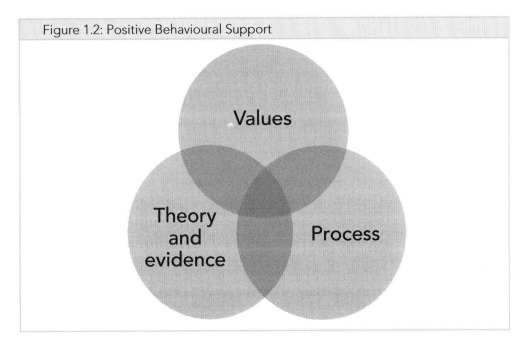

Figure 1.2: Positive Behavioural Support

Values

There are a number of values that are central to PBS, including:

- normalisation (people want to live as 'normal' lives as possible)

- human rights (we need to pay attention to everyone's basic and fundamental human rights at the forefront of any intervention)

- self-determination (people want to have choice and control over their life and decisions).

These values underpin how PBS is used and what outcomes we are interested in achieving.

Importantly, PBS aims to enhance quality of life as both an intervention and outcome for people who display behaviour that challenges and those who support them. PBS interventions are also constructional. That means that there is a large emphasis on increasing the person's skills, abilities and life opportunities, for example teaching someone to learn new skills or to better communicate their needs, such as asking for a break in place of behaviour that challenges. The use of punitive or restrictive approaches is completely rejected on the basis that it goes against these core values.

PBS takes account of the behaviour and well-being of the individual as well as their network (such as paid supporters and family carers), and it emphasises participation to ensure that assessments, interventions and outcomes are meaningful. PBS is therefore 'done with' rather than 'done to' the person and those who support them.

Theory and evidence base

PBS is based on an understanding that behaviours that challenge serve important functions for those who display them. As described above, behaviours develop and are maintained within the context of a person's abilities, needs (including their physical and mental health) and life circumstances. The characteristics of the social and physical environment need to be considered carefully.

This understanding, together with many of the assessment and intervention methods used in PBS, is grounded in behavioural theory described above, often referred to as applied behavioural analysis. PBS is an inclusive approach that uses additional evidence-based approaches that are in line with its values and planned outcomes, such as individual therapy from psychology, speech and language therapy and occupational therapy etc.

The PBS process

PBS requires assessment and support arrangements to be personalised and grounded directly in information that has been gathered about the person (including their broader needs and abilities) and their environment. The PBS process begins with a systematic assessment of when, where, how and why an individual displays behaviour that challenges. This process is known as functional assessment, or functional analysis. This involves:

1. A clear description of the behaviours of concern.

2. Identifying the events, times and situations that predict when the behaviour will and will not occur across the person's full range of typical daily routines. This might include observation or interview.

3. Identifying the consequences that maintain the behaviour.

4. Developing one or more summary statements that include the information above to give a hypothesis about the function of the behaviours of concern.

PBS plan

Behaviour that challenges will often occur for a number of reasons (or serve a number of functions). Any intervention therefore needs to target a number of these possible causes, for example a combination of adjustments to the environment, improving communication and increasing quality and quantity of interaction. This will form the basis of *proactive strategies* for a PBS plan.

A PBS plan will also describe an appropriate and ethical range of *reactive strategies* to guide responses to incidents of behaviour that are not preventable. These aim to prevent the behaviour getting worse and reduce the risk of harm to the person and others. At times, these may include physical interventions (see BILD, 2010) or medication[1], but these will only be used as a last resort and with careful planning. These should form a minority component of any plan, but they play a crucial role in terms of making people safe.

Case study: when staying 'safe' becomes restrictive

Jenny lives at home with her mother and sister. She has support for three hours at the weekend to go swimming. Jenny loves to go out and often dislikes coming home, and over the past few months she has run away when she was about to return home. On one occasion Jenny ran across a busy road, and on another she ran into a local park and it took a few hours to find her and support her to come home. Jenny's mother and sister are very worried she may be harmed as a result of her behaviour. The support worker who works with her on Saturdays doesn't think it's safe to support Jenny to access the community anymore and as a result Jenny is now no longer going out on Saturdays.

In this example we can hypothesise that the function of Jenny's behaviour is to stay out in the community longer. However, due to concerns about her safety and the impact on others, the measure put in place actually restricts her further, limits her access to the community and has a negative impact on her quality of life. This is a common example of how restrictive practices can be put in place to manage perceived risk.

---

1   For more information, see STOMP policy (www.vodg.org.uk/campaigns/stompcampaign/)

For more information, refer to Chapter 15 on positive risk taking, which emphasises the importance of supporting individuals with learning disabilities to take positive risks in order to achieve their goals and wishes.

Case study: PBS in practice

Background

Ola has a significant learning disability and autism. She is in her 40s and has always lived at home with her family. She is well known to the local learning disability teams and has received a service over the years to support behaviour considered challenging. The current referral was made by Ola's social worker as her mother had a fall and was no longer able to support her at home. Ola's social worker was supporting her and her family to consider a longer term plan, and Ola was due to move from the family home to a supported living placement.

Description of behaviour that challenges

Ola has a history of self-injurious behaviour including biting her hand, hitting her head with her fist and banging her head against the wall. She has also been physically aggressive towards others, such as hitting people with her fists or kicking them. Ola has a behavioural support plan in place, however given the change in her living situation, her family and support team have requested support to revise this plan and consider the most helpful way to support Ola at the moment.

Assessment

Following a full physical health check, which ruled out any physical health difficulties, a functional assessment was completed by behavioural support staff, speech and language therapists and occupational therapists at the learning disability team. This included a clear description of the behaviours of concern, interviews with family and support workers (using the functional assessment interview), monitoring of behaviour (using ABC charts) and completion of an outcome measure called the CBI. Behavioural support staff also spent a lot of time with Ola and her family completing direct observations and gaining a good understanding of when, how, with whom and under what circumstances the behaviour happened, as well as considering her overall activity and interactions throughout the day.

Based on this functional assessment, the following formulation was made of the behavioural difficulties. This formulation was based on the three areas outlined in Figure 1.1 on p18: vulnerabilities, maintaining processes and impact.

Formulation

Vulnerability

In terms of her 'vulnerabilities', Ola is a woman with a significant learning disability and limited verbal communication skills. She has long-standing behavioural difficulties that had been learned and reinforced throughout her life and, in the context of a change in living situation, her behaviour had become increasingly difficult to manage.

Maintaining process

It was hypothesised that the function of Ola's behaviour was to gain access to food and drink and to avoid social interaction. Ola's behaviour was also more likely to challenge if she had not slept or if there were changes to her daily routine, such as alterations to activities or staffing. It was therefore considered that the current change within her family home could have an impact on her behaviour.

When Ola engaged in self-injurious behaviours or aggression, it was likely that she would gain access to food and drink, and it was also effective at reducing social demand – that is, family and staff withdrew interaction. As such, Ola had learned over time that these behaviours were effective, and other ways to communicate these needs were not understood or went noticed.

Impact

The impact of these behaviours was that her quality of life was compromised. She had little meaningful engagement in activities and very few positive interactions. She spent a lot of time alone.

Intervention

A joint formulation from the health team was shared with Ola and her family, and a PBS plan was jointly designed. This plan placed a lot of emphasis on proactive strategies, based on the above formulation.

The plan included helping Ola to understand her environment and routine, including possible demands or changes, by introducing a visual timetable. Staff were encouraged to think about possible activities that may be meaningful and enjoyable for Ola. Staff were then encouraged to think and plan possible activities, including how they would be introduced, how long they would last and how to communicate when they would finish. Staff were supported to think about the possible advantages and disadvantages of spending increased time with Ola. They were also encouraged to consider Ola's quality of life and to discuss any fears they had about changing their current ways of supporting Ola.

Particular emphasis was placed on supporting staff to notice any communication that Ola used to tell them that she wanted to finish or have a break. The aim of this was to increase the amount of positive interaction between staff and Ola as a means to support both Ola and staff to enjoy spending time together.

A clear transition plan for Ola moving to new supported living accommodation was made including training for new support workers.

As part of the PBS plan, reactive strategies were also considered. These included very clear guidance of how to respond to behaviour that challenges. It was emphasised that a lot of energy and support needed to be dedicated to proactive strategies, however at times it would be necessary to respond to behavioural difficulties. The key principle of reactive guidance is to notice early and respond as quickly as possible. Ola had an individualised reactive response plan that clearly outlined the behaviours to look out for and how to respond to them, for example when Ola began to increase vocalising and biting the back of her hand, she should be given a break.

Figure 1.3: Positive behaviour support
To positively support student behaviour, the team must work together.

Target behaviour	Observations	Data collection
Function (To get... / To avoid...)	Replacement behaviour	Interventions (Teach, Cue, Prompt, Model)
Reinforcement	Implement the plan	Continue the process

Outcome

The main outcome of this intervention was that Ola's level of interaction with staff, and the level of her inclusion in meaningful interactions increased significantly. Staff also reported that they enjoyed spending time with Ola more and, as a result, the intervention could be maintained.

Ola moved to her new supported living accommodation and had an increased range of activities. There are still occasional incidents of behaviour that challenges, however the severity and frequency of these have decreased. Overall, these changes have had a very positive effect on her quality of life.

Overview and summary

This chapter has described what we understand by the term 'behaviour that challenges', some of the causes and reasons behind it, and the potential impact of difficult to manage behaviours. It has outlined that there are times when efforts to manage behaviour become restrictive and can limit an individual's quality of life. As people supporting someone whose behaviour is described as challenging, the 'challenge' is to find a way to support that individual to achieve the best quality of life while supporting that person and others to stay safe and well. PBS is an approach to challenging behaviour that places the person's wishes and needs at the centre of what we do as carers, and supports that individual to have the best quality of life possible.

References

BILD (2010) BILD Code of Practice for the use and reduction of restrictive physical interventions. Kidderminster: BILD.

Emerson E (2001) *Challenging Behaviour: Analysis and intervention in people with learning disabilities* (2nd Edition). Cambridge: Cambridge University Press.

Gore NJ, McGill P, Toogood S, Allen D, Hughes JC, Baker P, Hastings RP, Noone SJ & Denne LD (2013) Definition and scope for positive behavioural support. International Journal of Positive Behavioural Support 3(2) 14–23.

Hastings RP, Allen D, Baker P, Gore NJ, Hughes JC, McGill P, Noone SJ & Toogood S (2013) A conceptual framework for understanding why challenging behaviours occur in people with developmental disabilities. *International Journal of Positive Behavioural Support* **3**(2) pp5–13.

NICE (2015) Learning Disabilities: Challenging behaviour (Quality standard QS101) [online]. Available at: https://www.nice.org.uk/guidance/qs101 (accessed September 2017).

Useful resources

PBS Academy: http://pbsacademy.org.uk/

BILD Video: http://www.bild.org.uk/capbs/pbsinformation/introduction-to-pbs/

STOMP policy: https://www.vodg.org.uk/campaigns/stompcampaign/

Harris J, Allen D, Cornick M, Jefferson A & Mills R (1996) *Physical Interventions: A policy framework*. Kidderminster: BILD.

Harris J, Cornick M, Jefferson A & Mills R (2008) *Physical Interventions:* A policy framework (2nd Edition). Kidderminster: BILD.

Chapter 3:

Communication

By Paula Abreu, Gill Concannon and Peter Woodward

Aims

- To understand the skills that go into communication.

- How we can facilitate communication for a person so they express their needs more effectively.

- To understand the challenges relating to communication faced by people with learning disabilities.

Summary

Communication is essential to our everyday lives. It fosters good relationships and allows us to express our needs, wishes and disapproval. In this chapter, we consider the skills and needs of the individuals for whom we provide services, and our role in facilitating their communication to enable them to better express their wants, needs and views in their daily lives, using examples from education and health.

Introduction

This chapter will help the reader develop their understanding of, and skills in, communication. Communication is central to successful caring relationships and to effective team working. Listening is as important as what we say and do, and essential for 'no decision about me without me'. Communication is the key to a good workplace with benefits for those in our care and staff alike (DoH, 2012).

What is communication?

Communication may be simply described as the transference of information from one place to another, but on closer inspection the act of human communication is much more complex. Probably the first form of communication that will spring to mind for most people is verbal communication, however this is not used in isolation but simultaneously with other components of communication such as non-verbal communication, including listening, intonation, facial expression and body language, all of which enhance meaning.

To explore these components further, let's look at the key areas of verbal and non-verbal communication.

Verbal communication

Receptive language

Receptive language is the understanding of what is being said to you by another. It involves being able to understand a vocabulary of words and concepts, as well as how the order of words conveys meaning. Knowledge of sentence structure and grammatical rules are a factor in being able to follow what is being said, as is being able to retain all the information in order to be able to process it and take meaning from it. In order to respond to verbal information, an individual therefore has to be able to hear and attend to the relevant language (selectively filtering out other noise), and to have a fundamental understanding that words and the meanings they convey.

Expressive language

Expressive language involves our ability to select relevant words and organise them in to different sequences in order to convey meaning to a listener. Utterances become more sophisticated as more words are combined together, and sentence structure follows conventional grammatical rules. Increased length and complexity enable the communication of more detail.

Speech

This term refers to the ability to produce speech sounds appropriate to the language being used, and to combine motor speech articulatory patterns to make words that are clear in order to communicate meaning to a listener. Prosodic features also need to be considered here, which are factors that impact on meaning but are not speech sounds, i.e. pitch, intonation and stress patterns in words.

Fluency

This label refers to the flow with which sounds, syllables, words and phrases are joined together when speaking. 'Dysfluency' is any break in fluent speech and can be characterised by blocking, prolongations and the repetition of sounds, syllables or words. The terms 'stammering' and 'stuttering' are commonly used to describe dysfluent speech.

Non-verbal communication

Non-verbal communication describes those components of communication that convey meaning but that do not involve speech. This includes body language, gesture, facial expression and eye contact. Body language can convey meaning and emotion through body posture and movements, and can be conscious or unconscious. Gesture is specific to the movement of part of the body, especially a hand or the head to express an idea, feeling or meaning. Natural gesture is culturally defined, but gestures can be extended into communication signing systems which can convey meaning to a very complex level, so becoming its own language.

Facial expression as a term describes the movement and positions of the facial muscles in order to form expressions that convey particular emotional states. Eye contact – i.e. the act of directly looking into another's eyes – is seen to be meaningful in communication and can communicate a range of things from attentiveness and interest in what is being said to anger or aggression. These elements can be evident in isolation or used in combination with verbal skills to add to the message conveyed.

Communication difficulties in individuals with a learning disability

'*Up to 90% of people with a learning disability have communication difficulties; with half having significant difficulties.*' (Royal College of Speech and Language Therapists (RCSLT), 2013)

Communication difficulties in adults with learning disabilities can include:

- Sensory impairments e.g. hearing/visual impairment.
- Difficulties understanding language, writing and symbols, and interpreting environmental sounds.
- Having an insufficient vocabulary to express a range of needs, ideas or emotions.
- Being unable to formulate a sentence.
- Difficulties maintaining focus and concentration in order to communicate.
- Dysfluency e.g. stammering.
- Being unable to articulate clearly, which may be due to physical factors.
- Impaired social skills, which may prevent positive interactions with people.

Many people with a learning disability may experience some or all of the communication challenges listed above and these challenges can impact the way a person understands information and how they communicate. They may, for example, be unable to follow simple instructions, struggle to understand given information, or they may have difficulty in reading and/or interpreting signage. It is often the case that, as communication difficulties increase, behaviours that are considered challenging typically increase in frequency, intensity and duration. In these instances, many people with learning disabilities are dependent on others to support them for good communication.

Ways to support individuals with a learning disability to communicate

Listed below are some communication strategies that can be useful when interacting with individuals who have communication difficulties. The effectiveness of each will be dependent on the needs of the individual person being supported and the particular situation and context, including the emotional state of those involved:

- Listen: give the person time to express themselves and take time to try and understand.

- Observe: observing non-verbal behaviour may give clues as to emotional state.

- Reflect back in simple terms what you have understood about what they are communicating.

- Paraphrase what they have said to gain greater clarity, if appropriate.

- Summarise by giving the main points communicated if relevant.

- Use visual materials to support emotional regulation and communication, e.g. visual schedules, now/next schedules, rules and social cues.

- Use communications systems such as picture exchange systems or communication books, pictures, photos or physical gestures or signs.

- Define the time that an activity will take.

- Model context-specific language.

- Stay calm.

- Attune to a person's emotional state.

- One person to take control.

- Allow plenty of personal space.

- Offer a choice of what to do.

- Find a calming activity if the person is agitated.

- Keep your body language calm.

- Offer praise when you get compliance.

The following case studies illustrate interventions to enhance understanding and communication.

Case study: James

James is an eight-year-old boy with a diagnosis of Down's syndrome. He is placed in a special needs centre that is attached to a mainstream junior school. Staff at the school also feel that James presents with features of autistic spectrum disorder, but this is currently undiagnosed. His communication profile is as follows:

Listening and attention: James has a short attention span and is often distracted by his own agenda.

Receptive language: James is not always able to engage with verbal language. He is not able to cope with long utterances and he needs simple instructions given with time to process and respond.

Expressive language: James is able to use utterances of two words together consistently, and can use some three-word utterances in more structured settings.

Speech: James' speech production is impacted by general low muscle tone, characteristic of individuals with Down's syndrome, so speech can be unclear and difficult to follow, particularly out of context.

Communication skills: James has limited use of meaningful eye contact. He will initiate communication with adults by using gestures that involve physical manipulation (i.e. pulling a caregiver's hand) and pulling them to where he wants them to see what he wants, rather than a gesture to send a 'shared message' (i.e. pointing, showing, waving).

James has poorly developed functional communication skills and finds it hard to use language to express his needs, such as requesting, commenting and interaction through conversation. It can be difficult to engage him in learning tasks directed by adults and his behaviour can be challenging. He can be physical at times and rough with peers, and he has little insight into others' perspectives or views.

Scenario

James has been having his lunch at the table in his special needs centre. Having finished eating, he wants to get out of his chair and he begins to push against the table to get out (he is motivated by the fact that his usual routine is to play on a computer during the break time). Two staff start using verbal language simultaneously in an attempt to influence his behaviour, giving long utterances asking James to wait and listing the reasons why he should. He continues to struggle and pushes at the table, which other children are sitting at, tipping over a cup of water that was on the table. He manages to get out of his chair and makes a grab for a computer which an adult holds out of reach and they move across the room to a work bench. James is quite agitated and the staff member continues to talk to him giving an explanation that she is about to set up the computer. Once the computer is up and running James settles and becomes absorbed in the familiar activity and becomes calmer.

Thinking about James's case, consider the following questions:

■ What strategies could be helpful when dealing with James?

■ How could the staff members have reacted differently in this situation?

■ How did you rate practice in relation to the needs of this individual?

Case study: Ollie

Ollie is a 15-year-old boy in a special school for pupils with learning and additional needs. He does not have a specific diagnosis but has a learning disability with significant speech and language difficulties. His communication profile is as follows:

Listening and attention: Ollie has to work hard to sustain his attention and needs frequent adult reminders to focus on the task.

Receptive language: He has significant memory and language processing difficulties. His vocabulary knowledge is limited.

Expressive language: Ollie is able to use verbal language to express himself with simple sentences, and occasionally with some more complex sentences e.g. using 'because'.

Speech: He has poor speech intelligibility and tends to mumble and speak very quickly when unfocused, which can be difficult to follow out of context.

Communication skills: Ollie uses good eye contact when focused. He is not always able to interpret other people's non-verbal communication such as their body language or gestures. He initiates interaction with peers and adults on occasion but can be passive. Ollie's functional communication skills are developing and he can express his needs, such as requesting, commenting and interaction through conversation in familiar situations. It can be difficult for him to engage in his learning environment and he can become anxious and relies on adult support.

Scenario

Ollie has gone with his tutor group to his local college for sessions as part of his KS4 school curriculum. He is standing in the entrance hall with his group, waiting to go in to a particular course for the morning when he is approached by his regular teaching assistant (TA) who has noticed that he was looking anxious and agitated. After a conversation it is discovered that Ollie has left his lunch in his locker at school. The TA is able to reassure him that he is able to buy a sandwich in the canteen and that his problem can be resolved.

In Olllie's case, what strategies can you list that may have been used in this scenario?

What would the TA need to do/have available during this session away from school?

Communication problems in healthcare settings

In everyday situations people with learning disabilities find themselves in they will be exposed to jargon. Although assisting or supporting someone with communication is a transferable skill, the support someone requires may differ according to the setting. So far we have looked at education. The section below looks at how a person's support needs may change in different environments. Some examples of the issues that may arise in a medical or care setting are provided next and the challenges that can present when communicating with doctors and other health professionals.

Communication problem: jargon

People with learning disabilities may have difficulty understanding medical jargon or technical terms. They may use the word 'tummy' rather than 'stomach' or 'poo' rather than 'faeces'.

Just like anyone else, people with learning disabilities may not want to look foolish and may pretend that they understand when they do not. They may say 'yes' or 'no' to everything because they do not understand what they are being asked.

They may agree with the person questioning them, especially if they see them as being in power, wearing a badge or if they have a uniform like a paramedic or nurse. This can be a problem if they are asked a leading question such as, 'So, you have a pain in your left leg?', resulting in the individual replying, 'yes'.

Solutions

Communication aids can be used to help increase the understanding of what is being said. These could be pictures or models of body parts that can be pointed to. The spoken word can be backed up by pointing, gesturing or using sign language.

An answer can be verified by asking it again later or reversing the question to check that the correct answer was given the first time. For example, if the individual said they had a pain on the right side of their chest, later they can be asked where they said the pain was or to point to where the pain is to confirm. It is important to wait to do this because if the repeat question is asked immediately it will sound like they were not believed and the individual may deliberately change their answer.

Leading questions need to be avoided too. Instead of saying, 'It looks like you're having trouble gripping that cup, is your hand hurting?' one should simply ask if they are in pain at all or if there is a problem.

Communication problem: long sentences

Sentences need to be short without too many clauses in them. For example, giving lots of options can be confusing for a person with learning disabilities, and they may just choose the last thing on a list because they are confused by the number of options.

For example, if a nurse said, 'I think this may be due to the side effects of your medication. We have a few options here: you can stay on the medication and see if this is still affecting you tomorrow, you can make an appointment with your GP and ask him to try something new, as there are other options available, we could give your GP a call now and explain that you want to stop taking them, or you could try taking the tablets after dinner and see if this helps at all…'. There is far too much information being given here and the person may just choose the last option as a result.

Solution

If there is a long list of options, present these two at a time, let the individual choose one and then take this option and include a new one until all of the options have been explored.

For example, if there are three options (1) going to accident and emergency, (2) visiting the doctor in the morning, or (3) taking some paracetamol and seeing if the pain subsides, present the first two options first – 'Would you like to go to accident and emergency or wait to go to see the doctor in the morning?' If they say that they want to go to the doctor in the morning, then add the next choice – 'Ok, would you like to go to the doctor in the morning or take paracetamol now?'

Communication problems: abbreviations

Someone may have problems understanding medical abbreviations such as p.r.n., BMI, mg, BP or NHS. Other abbreviations can cause problems, especially when they are written down, such as 'e.g.', 'can't', 'etc.', 'Dr'. There can also be confusion around the use of 'negative words' such as 'don't', 'can't', 'won't' and 'isn't'.

Solutions

Abbreviations should be spoken in full, avoiding confusing negatives. For example, instead of saying 'don't go to the clinic after five o'clock; it isn't open,' say, 'Go to the clinic before five when it is open'. Active verbs should also be used, so instead of saying, 'You told me that the day centre was where you had an asthma attack,' you might instead say, 'You told me you had an asthma attack at the day centre'.

Use nouns rather than pronouns. For example, instead of saying, 'Your **appointment** [noun] will be at ten o'clock. **It** [pronoun] is with Doctor Smith and **it** [pronoun] will last 30 minutes.' Instead, use '**Your appointment** will be at ten o'clock. **Your appointment** will be with Doctor Smith. **Your appointment** will last 30 minutes.' This feels a lot more long-winded, but it is easier to understand.

Clear and precise messages are crucial.

Other points to remember

Remembering illness progression

It can be difficult for people with learning disabilities to remember when an illness or problem started, or when symptoms were first noticed or they got worse.

The use of 'anchor events' can help someone recall information. Instead of asking, 'how long have you had the cough?', a professional might instead ask: 'Have you had the cough since you last went out/I last visited/since your holiday/losing your job?' Choosing a recent event helps to anchor the event in time for the individual.

Rating scales

Beware of using rating scales, such as, 'Tell me out of ten how much it hurts'. This can sometimes be difficult for someone to describe.

Sometimes 'smiley' or 'sad' faces are used instead, with the person with learning disabilities asked to point at the picture that best describes how they feel. The practitioner needs to ensure, however, that they are not just pointing to the 'happy face' because that's the picture they like best.

The written word

Sometimes people will need written instructions, for example to remind them when they have a dentist appointment or when to take their medication. There are a few things that can help with this.

First, use of numerals for numbers, not words. So, for example, write 'Take 2 tablets at 9 o'clock' rather than 'Take two tablets at nine o'clock'.

When referring to your service, use the term 'we' and when talking about the individual being addressed, use the term 'you'. Example: 'We need you to go to the clinic on Tuesday morning.'

Pictures or symbols should be included to back up written words. The pictures should be on the left and the writing on the right. The same picture should be used to mean the same thing, rather than having lots of meanings because it is used to describe a number of situations.

Lots of punctuation should be avoided but full stops are acceptable.

A large font (18 point or above) should be used with a simple font design like 'Arial'.

Advice from a speech and language therapist should be sought.

Easyhealth have lots of advice and some videos on several health conditions relating to people with learning disabilities. These can be found at: http://www.easyhealth.org.uk/

(All communication advice adapted from Hardy *et al*, 2010)

Summary

Individuals with communication difficulties can be seriously disadvantaged when they access health services, where it is necessary to provide information about health history, symptoms, medications and other conditions. As a result, health needs are often overlooked and avoidable mistakes can occur when common diseases and conditions are overlooked or put down to a person's disability. Behaviours seen as 'challenging' may be an expression of pain, and if attributed to the person's learning disability the complaint will be left untreated. This is known as diagnostic overshadowing.

It is therefore important to be aware of the communication needs of an individual. Plans that are in place to enable effective communication, such as using Makaton, gestures, symbols, Easy Read and objects of reference are all useful tools that can make communication easier. Staff need the skills to facilitate engagement, involvement and inclusion. Health services can minimise and reduce issues that contribute to communication difficulties and provide reasonable adjustments that may be needed.

Families and carers are a valuable resource for health services as they possess the expertise relating to the individual patient's communication needs. They can help by sharing communication plans and advice on how the individual they support communicates. Community learning disability teams often have speech and language therapists and other professionals who can advise and assist with communication strategies and supports. This provides people with learning disabilities the best chance of securing the rights, inclusion, choice and independence to which they are entitled.

Communication is an important aspect of our working life too. We must pay attention to how we communicate with our colleagues as miscommunication is often the root cause of difficulties within a team. By its nature, the nursing profession is generally described as particularly stressful (Demerouti *et al*, 2000; Hamaideh & Ammouri, 2011; Sundin *et al*, 2011). This appears to be especially problematic if nurses are detached and withdrawn from their co-workers, and not able to communicate sufficiently in challenging situations. Be mindful of the gestures, words and body language you use when interacting with people at work. Reflect on a person you get on well with. How do you greet them? What is your body language like? What is your facial expression? Now ask yourself the same questions for someone you do not engage with well. Reflect further, could you make some minor adjustments to your actions? Could you make the team stronger by acting in a professional manner and adjusting your actions and the way in which you communicate?

References

Demerouti E, Bakker AB, Nachreiner F & Schaufeli WB (2000) A model of burnout and life satisfaction amongst nurses. *Journal of Advanced Nursing* **32** 454–464.

Department of Health (2012) *Libertaing the NHS: No decision about me, without me*. London: DoH.

Hamaideh SH & Ammouri A (2011) Comparing Jordanian nurses' job stressors in stressful and non-stressful clinical areas. *Contemporary Nurse* **37** 173–187.

RCSLT (2013) *Five Good Communication Standards*. Royal College of Speech and Language Therapists.

Sundin L, Hochwälder J & Lisspers J (2011) A longitudinal examination of generic and occupational specific job demands, and work-related social support associated with burnout among nurses in Sweden. *Work: A journal of prevention, assessment and rehabilitation* **38** 389–400.

Chapter 4:

From advocacy to involvement to co-production and back again

By Thomas Doukas

Aims

The aim of this chapter is to help understand advocacy and involvement as creative and imaginative means for organisations and the public sector to shift the balance of decision-making power in favour of people with learning disabilities and their families.

The title of this chapter was inspired by the title of Andy Warhol's book *The Philosophy of Andy Warhol (From A to B and Back Again)*. Warhol claimed that he loved being outside a party so that he could get in. Whether you call it advocacy, involvement, engagement or co-production, I think the best place to start is looking at it from the outside and then get in…

Summary

This chapter explores the notions of advocacy, involvement and co-production. These three interconnected terms all have very similar functions and scope, and ultimately their aim is to create a process by which people are able to be actively and genuinely involved in defining the issues that concern them, and also to become integral to making decisions and acting to implement changes that affect their lives, by influencing policies, planning and the development and delivery of services.

Advocacy – the basic and the most essential process of giving people with learning disabilities a voice – has developed into the concept of involvement, a more solid form of user engagement that incorporates a full range of people's experiences, from sharing information to planning and developing services. Co-production is an extension of involvement and entails services that are delivered through equal and reciprocal relationships between professionals and people using the service and their relatives, and which are designed to make the most of everybody's experiences and strengths to achieve better outcomes.

Advocacy

Advocacy is the process of supporting and enabling people, especially those who are most vulnerable in society, to have their voices heard and their views and wishes expressed when decisions are being made about their lives. Advocacy seeks to defend and safeguard people's rights, and to consider their position by exploring choices. An advocate can support a person or a group of people to access information, or attend meetings, write a letter on behalf of the person, or speak for them in situations in which the person doesn't feel able to speak for themselves.

Advocacy is a process of supporting and enabling people to:

- express their views and concerns
- access information and services
- defend and promote their rights and responsibilities
- explore choices and options.

So, in this sense, advocacy means getting support from another person to help express one's views and wishes, and to help make sure their voice is heard. Someone who acts as an advocate should have the person's best interests at heart.

Involvement

The term 'advocacy' has come to be closely related to involvement. In all its forms, involvement is an on-going and sustained process of collaboration and information sharing between a public body or organisation and people with an interest in their work. Involvement is a form of public engagement in decision-making that recognises that:

- all people and all communities have a right to help shape and influence decisions that affect them
- involving a range of individuals and groups in decision-making is valuable because it creates greater resources, gives clearer insights, more diverse perspectives and shared knowledge, ideas and experiences to draw on
- good involvement helps deliver better decisions, is a better use of resources, and gives better outcomes for participants, communities and organisations
- barriers to participation in involvement should be removed.

People at all levels are vital to an organisation, and their full involvement ensures their abilities can be used for everybody's benefit. Some key benefits are that:

- people are motivated, committed and involved
- innovation and creativity help to achieve objectives and outcomes
- people are accountable for their own decisions
- people are eager to participate in and contribute to continual improvement.

Applying the principle of involvement typically leads to people being able to:

- understand the importance of their contribution and role in the organisation and the decision-making process
- identify constraints to their performance
- accept ownership of problems and their responsibility for solving them
- evaluate their performance against their personal goals and objectives
- actively seek opportunities to enhance their competence, knowledge and experience
- freely share knowledge and experience
- openly discuss problems and issues.

Co-production

The term 'co-production' was coined as early as the late 1970s by Elinor Ostrom and colleagues at Indiana University to explain why neighbourhood crime rates went up in Chicago when the city's police officers spent more time in their cars rather than walking the streets. By 2004 the term was being used in the UK by voluntary and community organisations (VCOs) in the provision of public services (Osborne & McLaughlin, 2004). The term is used to imply the role of those organisations in the delivery of community services. The Care Act (2014) statutory guidance offers the following definition:

'"Co-production" is when an individual influences the support and services received, or when groups of people get together to influence the way that services are designed, commissioned and delivered.'

In 2015 the Social Care Institute of Excellence (SCIE) defined it as:

'... a key concept in the development of public services. It has the potential to make an important contribution to all of the big challenges that face social care services.'

In services for people with disabilities there are various levels of co-production, from providing one-to-one support (e.g. planning activities, health and well-being etc.) to community level co-production (e.g. developing new types of services and support that builds on social capital, such as peer support, time banks, coaching, mentoring, community connecting), to strategic level co-production (e.g. people co-designing, co-commissioning and co-delivering outcomes).

One way or the other, what the term 'co-production' really infers is that the involvement of the third sector, or charitable organisations, transforms the delivery of public services. This relationship between the third sector and the production process is a dynamic one in that the involvement of stakeholders not only transforms the service but the stakeholders are transformed as well, as part of the process, in their expectations and understanding and in feeling empowered. At the same time, third-sector organisations deliver services differently, and in doing so they incorporate themselves into this transformation by adapting and evolving the services all the time to meet the person's needs.

Co-production is not just a term or a model – it is a dialogue-based approach, a coming together of minds to find a solution to a shared problem. In practice, it involves people who use services being consulted, included and collaborated with from the start to the end of any project that affects them (Think Local Act Personal, 2011).

When people begin working with a co-production approach, there are a number of things that they need to consider in relation to the individuals they will be involved with:

- Mindset: they need to have a good understanding of the fundamentals of human rights, group dynamics, personal differences and relationships.
- Recruitment: they will need to identify the individual skills they are looking for in people with learning disabilities; provide training; offer opt in/out options; set clear goals and expectations; and ideally introduce a payment scheme.
- Design: they will need to identify the skills and roles they are looking for; explore methodologies for working together; decide on research or working topics.
- Accessibility: the service will need to be accessible to support contributions from people with learning disabilities and help with their learning.
- Practicalities: how will the stakeholders travel to and from locations; will there be flexible timeframes for working; what support needs will the stakeholders require.

■ Gathering, analysing and sharing information: how will information be accessible and how will discussion be facilitated at all stages? How are new ideas and experiences to be shared?

Key point: with co-production should come equity

Let's be clear, it is not acceptable anymore to involve people with learning disabilities without paying them. If we can pay the co-ordinator of any scheme involving people, then we can pay the people who take part, be it a consultation, quality checking, research, or anything else. In a recent conference in Scotland, one self-advocate said:

'You are expecting and inviting people with disabilities to share their experiences and expertise for free while other professionals who get paid for their professional opinions and as a result they have a better quality of life, are sitting at the very same table with disabled people. We are lucky if we get free lunch or a posh biscuit or M&S vouchers. Co-production the way it is done, is fundamentally dishonest because the power dynamics are so skewed towards one group.'

The second issue that needs to be considered is the outcomes:

■ Make it worthwhile for the individual: give them new experiences and opportunities to learn and develop skills, to grow and take responsibility, to get recognition to be treated as equal colleagues.

■ Learn from the other side: this is a chance to listen to peoples' views; to get new insights and information and to discover what's important to people with learning disabilities; to learn new and creative ways of communicating.

■ Benefits for the industry: urgent issues can be highlighted and can be better understood; better support and fitting care can be provided and services can be improved.

■ Benefits for the community: reduces inequalities; raises awareness; influences change.

The level of support needed will depend on the needs of the individual. For example, in the London South Bank University People's Academy, experts by experience from all walks of life are employed to develop courses, deliver teaching and training, present at conferences and work on consultancy projects. To support members to participate they will work with other university staff and work either independently or with support and/or supervision from others.

Case studies

Case study 1: choice without information is no choice at all

Sally attends the annual general meeting of a small organisation in her local area that provides leisure activities for people with disabilities. She gets there with her supporter. Sally has attended the activities provided by this organisation for years and in the past she has also volunteered to help with the activities. At the annual general meeting the organisers ask people if they want to become members of the committee. The organisers explain briefly about the commitments for the members and payment, and what the committee does, but Sally doesn't understand all of it and it's all happened too fast. Echoing the initial announcement made by the event organiser, Sally's supporter simply asks Sally the same question: 'Do you want to become a member of the committee?'. Sally replies, 'No'.

Thinking activity

Imagine you were Sally's supporter and consider the following points:

1. Think about open and closed questions and how best to phrase the question.
2. Think about how you might ask the question and explain what it's all about. For example, you might give examples of some aspects of it, share your own experiences or explain what the committee members do etc.
3. Expand and reflect together. For example, ask Sally what she thinks it is and discuss it with her.

Case study 2: 'Meaningful' is the word

Mark lives in a flat with two other people where they get support around the clock. Mark and his housemates need help with almost all aspects of their daily lives, from getting up and ready in the morning, to preparing meals and going to activities. The manager of this service wants to give all the residents the power to make decisions about their home by establishing a residents' meeting. To do this in a non-tokenistic way, the manager makes the meeting fun and discusses only one or two items with the residents giving different options so the residents understand their choices. For example, when the residents needed to decide what sofa they would like to buy for their shared living room, the manager supported the residents to explore different options by looking at a furniture brochure and cutting out the pictures of the sofas they liked most before they decided which one to buy.

Discussion topics at these meetings need to be meaningful for the people involved, and less complex topics do not lessen the involvement of people with learning disabilities or the importance of having the meeting. Meaning is personal and varies from person to person.

Thinking activity

1. Think about minutes from the meeting – if the residents cannot use the minutes, is there any point having minutes at all?

2. Think about creating an alternative format to document the meeting e.g. use big pictures and then attach them to a large sheet of paper or a big book as evidence of the meeting. Remember, this is only ok if it's meaningful to the people in this house.

3. Think of practical ways to make the meeting accessible. For example, use big pictures of the topic and the choices the residents want to explore; use thumbs-up and thumbs-down pictures to facilitate choice.

Key learning points and opportunities for reflection

Whether you call it advocacy, involvement, engagement or co-production, to be authentic and fruitful it must be built on good relationships, which are themselves built on trust. And trust takes time! On the other hand, to be meaningful one must take into consideration all minute details of the specific individual or group it aims to involve.

This chapter has explained some of the key features of co-production and involvement – features we all know well. We've heard it all before... So, why does it take us so long to implement these approaches?

Meaningful involvement needs to be a priority from the first steps of honest conversation and openness, and it needs to be driven by the appetites of professionals and people with disabilities and their families to come together and work collaboratively. If these foundations are not solid or non-existent, then co-production is unlikely to work.

Being honest and clear about the status of an organisation's involvement practice (how much/well are people involved?) is an important first step, and it's vital to have this conversation, laying the foundations to move forward and face the challenges that lie ahead.

Building relationships and bridges takes times and resources, and even more to maintain them. Quick fixes through tokenistic involvement exercises and rushed efforts will not address the complex issues social care is facing. To quote Theodore Roosevelt: 'Do what you can, with what you have, where you are'. This is evidently the most effective way to implement change. Meaningful involvement and co-production is an opportunity to create better outcomes for people as well as to achieve more creative approaches.

So, going back to the inspiration of the title of this chapter, a combination of a fresh pair of eyes and in-depth understanding of the issues involved is what's needed. Looking from the outside in, you can never understand it. Standing on the inside looking out, you can never explain it.

References

Osborne S & McLaughlin K (2004) The cross-cutting review of the voluntary sector: where next for local government - voluntary sector relationships? *Regional Studies* **38** 573–582.

Frankena TK, Naaldenberg J, Cardol M, Linehan C & van Schrojenstein Lantman-de Valk H (2015) Active involvement of people with intellectual disabilities in health research – a structured literature review. *Research in Developmental Disabilities* **45–46** 271–283.

Think Personal, Act Local (2011) *Making it Real: Marking progress towards personalised, community based support* [online]. Available at: https://www.thinklocalactpersonal.org.uk/_assets/NEWMakingItReal.pdf (accessed January 2018).

Chapter 5:

Sexuality and relationships education for people with learning disabilities

By Mark Brown

Aims

- To highlight the need for appropriate rights-based sex and relationship education for people with learning disabilities.

- To discuss key areas of need for people with learning disabilities.

- To encourage services for people with learning disabilities to consider the effectiveness of their sex and education programmes and approaches.

Summary

The sexuality of people with learning disabilities is often ignored. Although sex education for people with learning disabilities is considered taboo and still met with suspicion by some elements of the community, it is essential in helping people to learn about their bodies, health, development and what are healthy relationships. This helps keep them safe and healthy.

Introduction

Historically, the issue of sexuality and sexual needs in regard to individuals with learning disabilities has been ignored. Consequently, as mainstream sex education programmes have developed over the years, sex education for individuals with learning disabilities has been significantly less productive. The movement to rectify this situation finally took off in the 1970s through the work of a number of key players (e.g. Brown, 1994; Craft, 1994; McCarthy & Thompson, 2010), and has gradually developed with time. However, although progress has been made, there are still a number of barriers to overcome. These include:

- staff attitudes

- a lack of appropriate teaching materials

- specific issues related to people with autistic spectrum disorder (ASD)

- further adaptations that are required for people with ASD.

In the meantime, people with learning disabilities are too often ill-informed about their sexual development, their rights, and how they can keep themselves safe while exploring this aspect of their lives. Difficulties occur in discussions around these issues as many people who support individuals with learning disabilities find the topics embarrassing, and as a result they are often avoided altogether, which can lead to frustration for individuals with learning disabilities and can put them at greater risk.

Good sex education

Comprehensive sex education programmes for these individuals is imperative in order to help overcome these issues and help the individual to deal with the world around them. In doing so, we reduce the individual's vulnerability while increasing their knowledge and understanding.

However, it is important to ask precisely what constitutes good sex education and how we effectively respond to sexual issues. An important starting point is to recognise that the rights of an individual with a learning disability to understand and express their sexuality are the same as for any other person, although there are legal differences and considerations to be made in regard to consent. While there are individuals for whom thoughts and feelings about these issues are not present due to being asexual, many people with learning disabilities will experience the same needs as anyone else; to have sexual relations, to enjoy relationships with girlfriends or boyfriends or to get married and have children.

Implementing good sex and relationship education (SRE) should be based upon a healthy, values-based approach aimed at providing accurate information that helps the individual with learning disabilities to develop appropriate social competencies to enjoy life while remaining safe. Such implementation needs to be as individualised as possible, taking into account any religious or cultural issues that may be present. This individualisation does not necessarily require one-to-one support, although in some situations the group environment may not be appropriate, but it is important to consider the composition of groups, for example classes or years might be split according to gender, culture or levels of ability.

It is important to note that in regard to this latter aspect, SRE should be available to all individuals with learning disabilities regardless of ability level. However, how that education is delivered with individuals classed as being unable to give legal consent will undoubtedly be different to how it is delivered to other, more able individuals. In these situations, the individual has the right to learn and understand how to say 'no', and to possess some recognition of inappropriate touching in order to keep safe.

Case study: John

John is a 19-year-old man with learning disabilities who attends a specialised unit within a mainstream college. Soon after joining the college, John expressed a wish to be a female. Initially, staff supported this idea without any discussion with John. However, John's parents requested specialist input, which discovered that John had not received any SRE programmes that incorporated discussions about sexual arousal and the opposite sex. These were subsequently provided. Consequently, through the sessions, John was able to understand that having an erection when around ladies he found attractive at the college did not mean that he wanted to be a woman. He verbalised within the sessions that his erections were to do with attraction rather than a need to be the opposite sex.

When implementing SRE, the content should include factual discussions about both the physical and social aspects of sexuality. This should use a range of methods to support learning, including videos, photographs and line drawings (Cambridge, 1997; McCarthy & Thompson, 2007), and language should be clear and unambiguous (Cambridge, 1997). There are a number of key areas to be considered in the implementation of an effective SRE programme.

(For more information, see the Further resources section on p211.)

Physical development

All individuals have a right and a need to understand their own physical development. SRE not only gives them knowledge about their bodies, but is also necessary when discussing other areas such as consent and the ability to say no if they understand that they are being touched inappropriately. Open and frank discussions surrounding physical development also assists with reproductive health. There is also a need to teach individuals with learning disabilities about certain issues regarding health screening, for example cervical or testicular cancer, just as we teach these things to the rest of society. The importance of recognising how the body develops and understanding issues that can arise are central to this right.

An important aspect regarding sexual health that is often overlooked is the need to prepare people to participate effectively in such health checks. Whether this is through social stories or individualised plans that provide both information and reassurance, without such preparation the experience for the individual with learning disabilities could be frightening and they might become anxious and traumatised by it.

(For more information see the Further resources section on p211.)

Case study: Danny

Danny is an 18-year-old man with a learning disability and autism. Danny had previously been in brief relationships with girls but concerns had been raised about his most recent, which seemed to be more serious. It was felt that the relationship may potentially become more intimate but that it was important for Danny to understand the concept of consent to ensure that he made the appropriate decisions. Consequently, Danny participated in an individualised SRE programme that explored all aspects of relationships, but which had a focus upon consent. As a result of the work, Danny was able to explore the situation in regard to his present relationship and in doing so he concluded that his girlfriend may not have had the understanding required to consent to sex. He therefore felt it appropriate to avoid a sexual relationship until his girlfriend had received input in regard to the situation.

Sexual health and contraception

Teaching and supporting people about their sexual health and contraception is a critical part of SRE. Although individuals with learning disabilities are not necessarily a high-risk group in relation to issues such as sexually transmitted infections, if engaging in high-risk sexual behaviour due to a lack of education, an individual with learning disabilities places both themselves and others in a vulnerable position.

Generally, for both genders the risks and consequences of pregnancy need to be explored, but more importantly, contraceptive methods for women with learning disabilities need to be considered and explored thoroughly. Too frequently the use of contraceptive methods, particularly oral medication, has been used under the guise of a blanket safety measure. Such approaches ignore the rights of the individual with learning disabilities and their human right to be informed in these decisions, and places too much importance upon the views of others. Once again, education and frank discussion are vital to the situation.

Wider socio-sexual world and issues of consent

For many individuals with learning disabilities, the wider socio-sexual concepts are rife with difficulties and dangers. Much of this danger comes from the shifting and sometimes unclear boundaries between acceptable and unacceptable behaviour, which people are confronted with on a daily basis, and which requires 'on the job' learning and adaptation. Discussions surrounding such issues should be aimed at promoting appropriate development and maintenance of relationships, including how to negotiate within relationships and ensuring that an individual's actions remain within legal parameters. However, for many with learning disabilities this is difficult without the appropriate guidance and places them in a vulnerable position, both in regard to being abused and to being an abuser.

Sexual abuse

Research has shown that sexual abuse of individuals with learning disabilities is a common occurrence. The reasons people with learning disabilities are vulnerable to this abuse include low self-esteem, a lack of societal value and living within environments where potential perpetrators could be present (e.g. staff and other people with learning disabilities). However, central to addressing this issue is knowledge acquired through appropriate education. Being able to understand the issues involved in keeping safe and developing appropriate relationships, as well as being able to recognise coercive and abusive situations, is difficult for many individuals with learning disabilities.

While for those individuals with more severe learning disabilities the issue of consent is a matter of law and therefore possesses more clarity, things are more difficult for those who have greater capacity to consent but do not have the knowledge they need. Informed consent involves the individual possessing the ability to fully comprehend what is being requested of them and what the consequences of their choices are. In relation to sexual and relationship issues, this requires the implementation of a comprehensive SRE programme that provides all the elements needed to make such decisions.

Internet and technology

As new technologies develop and come on the market, the ways in which we socialise change and evolve, which can lead to boundaries changing or becoming blurred. Furthermore, in the absence of good, reliable information, technology – and particularly the internet – has given people access to a wide range of other sources of information, many of which are inappropriate and have the potential to adversely affect individuals. This is why it is so important that these areas are addressed by support workers.

One of the ways that technology has impacted on people is through the greater ease of communication, with phones and social media that can connect people on a 24-hour basis. This can have a range of negative effects as it gives people with learning disabilities many more opportunities to socialise with others and potentially bring them into contact with predators or scammers, or they might find themselves being harassed or bullied. On the flip side of this, with access to a phone and the internet but without appropriate education, individuals with learning disabilities may find themselves responsible for making inappropriate contact with others or persisting in one-sided communication through texting and messaging that might be interpreted as harassment. There is also the issue of sexting and the dangers that this behaviour carries, which needs to be addressed.

Another risk that has become increased by the internet is the issue of pornography. Easy access to adult material can blur the lines of acceptable behaviour, or give very misleading impressions as to what sex and relationships entail. This may especially be the case, for example, if an individual is confronted with everyday situations that, in the pornography they have viewed, have led to sexual situations, and which leads them to engage in sexually inappropriate behaviour.

There is also a need to discuss the legalities of using the internet. Even within mainstream classrooms this area is often overlooked, but there are many issues that individuals with learning disabilities need to be made aware of in order to prevent them putting themselves in vulnerable positions or bringing them into contact with the criminal justice system. For example, issues around ages of consent, 'grooming' behaviour and child pornography need to be addressed, and people need to be kept up to date with any legal changes, such as the laws relating to 'revenge porn', for example, which has been made illegal only recently.

All of these issues are further impacted by the difficulties individuals with learning disabilities have in learning socio-sexual skills through more informal means, as well as often having limited opportunities to use the skills they do learn.

There are a range of effective resources that have been developed by organisations such as NSPCC which provide scenarios demonstrating these issues in a practical manner.

Summary and conclusion

This chapter has really just explored the tip of an iceberg, and the size and complexity of the subject requires greater discussion and exploration, particularly considering the ever-changing legal and social landscape in which we live. However, this author hopes that some of the issues highlighted in this chapter provide some guidance for the reader in order for them to effectively support individuals with learning disabilities to enjoy appropriate relationships.

As has been highlighted, the importance of providing comprehensive sex and relationship education programmes is a priority in keeping individuals with learning disabilities safe while also giving them the skills to develop appropriate intimate relationships within legal and social frameworks. Discussing such topics does not necessarily come naturally to many, but is a necessity and a right for everybody, including individuals with learning disabilities, and so it is imperative that people providing the support and knowledge overcome such inhibitions. Furthermore, those supporting people with learning disabilities need to look beyond the mainstream approaches and materials and 'think outside of the box' in order to develop and use material that meets the needs of the individuals they support. The more that people who support individuals with learning disabilities can put the advice in this chapter into action, the sooner the people they support can start enjoying this fundamental part of life.

References

Brown H (1994) 'An ordinary sexual life?' A review of the normalisation principle as it applies to the sexual options of people with learning disabilities. *Disability & Society* **9** (2).

Cambridge P (1997) At whose risk? Priorities and conflicts for policy development in HIV and intellectual disability. *Journal of Applied Research in Intellectual Disabilities* **10** (2).

Craft A (1994) *Practice Issues in Sexuality and Learning Disabilities*. Routledge.

McCarthy M & Thompson D (2007) Sex and the 3Rs: Rights, risks and responsibilities. *A sex education pack for working with people with learning disabilities*. Brighton: Pavilion Publishing and Media.

McCarthy M & Thompson D (2010) *Sexuality and Learning Disabilities: A handbook*. Brighton: Pavilion Publishing and Media.

Section 2:
Staying healthy

Chapter 6:

Health promotion and supporting people to access mental and physical health services

By Gill Concannon

Aims

- To introduce good practice in health promotion.
- To examine the barriers to health promotion for people with learning disabilities.
- To give examples of how to promote good physical and mental health successfully.

Summary

This chapter highlights some of the barriers currently experienced by people with learning disabilities in accessing healthcare and pinpoints factors that may hinder their inclusion in health promotion schemes. People with learning disabilities are more likely to die earlier than people in the general population. Central to the efforts of trying to address health inequalities are improvements to service experience to make them more inclusive, to improve communication and raise awareness of what it is like to have a learning disability. Examples of how to promote and improve the physical and mental well-being of people with learning disabilities are provided, including an exploration of some health promotion strategies that may be adopted.

Introduction

One priority of the Department of Health is to prevent ill health and support people to live healthier lives. Health promotion is 'the process of enabling people to increase control over their health, and its determinants, and thereby improve their health' (WHO, 2005). Health promotion focuses on a wide range of social and environmental interventions and its emphasis is both on individuals and communities. Health promotion strategies are not limited to a specific health problem, or to a specific set of behaviours, but rather are designed to promote a healthy lifestyle to bring about health benefits. Examples of promoting healthy lifestyles and providing a range of public health services include such initiatives as smoking cessation support, flu vaccination and NHS health screening checks.

Health promotion initiatives can be seen throughout society – in education, community development, policy, legislation and regulation – and each area is equally valid to promote positive well-being and to help prevent communicable diseases (CD) and non-communicable diseases (NCDs). CDs are defined as infectious diseases, transmissible (as from person to person) by direct contact with an affected individual or the individual's discharges, or by indirect means. NCDs, however, are defined as those diseases that are not transmissible or caused by injury: diseases such as cardiovascular diseases, which account for the deaths of 17.3 million people worldwide annually, followed by cancers (7.6 million), respiratory diseases (4.2 million), and diabetes (1.3 million). These four groups of diseases account for around 80% of all NCD deaths. NCDs often share common risk factors, which can be reduced through preventative strategies. They also often follow similar progressions and therefore can be supported by programmes with similar care or management approaches. In short, the question of why health promotion is necessary is made apparent by an examination of the key associated causal facts. NCDs kill more than 36 million people each year. They all share four risk factors: tobacco use, physical inactivity, the harmful use of alcohol and unhealthy diets.

It is well documented that inequalities in life expectancy and access to a healthy lifestyle persists between communities and groups (PHE, 2015). People with learning disabilities have among the poorest outcomes and die 16 years sooner on average than the general population and more than a third of these deaths are down to people not getting the right healthcare (DH, 2013). The issue of health inequality needs to be considered not only as one of social justice, but as one that adds hugely to NHS costs and to economic costs more widely. There is a compelling economic and social justice case for tackling health inequalities overall, but people with learning disabilities in particular have significantly poorer health than their non-disabled peers. In part this is because they have more difficulty in identifying important symptoms and getting access to appropriate care (Disability Rights Commission, 2006; Emerson *et al*, 2011; Mencap, 2007, 2012; Michael, 2008). There is, however, also an identified need for lifestyle improvement for people with learning disabilities which may be accomplished through health promotion and education.

What are the challenges and barriers to health promotion in LD?

Learning disability is 'a significantly reduced ability to understand new or complex information, to learn new skills with a reduced ability to cope independently, which started before adulthood, with a lasting effect on development' (DH, 2001). This definition offers some indication as to the vulnerabilities and possible difficulties a person may experience when faced with the abstract concept of health promotion or well-being in general. For example, there are often mixed messages in the media, such as the contradictory plethora of information that exists around diets and what is and is not good for us. Notably, despite the restrictions on misleading advertising put in place by the advertising regulator Ofcom in relation to food, broadcast advertising still plays a major role in publicity of unhealthy food in the UK (Cairns *et al*, 2013).

People with learning disabilities often rely on others for support in their daily lives, which means they also often rely on support from family members or staff for information about healthy living and for access to health care. Family carers and staff, however, may not possess adequate information to enable them to signpost others or they may be unaware of the facts themselves. People with learning disabilities may not have received relevant education and may have a limited understanding of healthy diets and the available options and alternatives. They may also lack the skills needed to prepare and cook nutritious, low-cost meals or know how to plan and budget.

This multi-faceted situation for people with learning disabilities is complex and exacerbated by such things as restricted incomes, not being in a position to purchase their own food or having no control over the food provided. Costly care packages may not include sufficient support time for the preparation and cooking of meals. In this way, fast food may become the staple diet for many. Dietary information may be complex and not available in formats that make it accessible, such as Easy Read format. Information that is very easily understood needs to be available in a number of mediums and for all groups of people with learning disabilities, for example those people for whom English is a second language or for those whose family carers struggle themselves with literacy.

It is also important to target the right people with the right information. For example, some syndromes that cause learning disabilities may also make the individual prone to obesity. In this instance, the health promotion message and education in healthy living with good diet and exercise is even more vital. It is therefore imperative that those in support roles are knowledgeable and well equipped to provide and facilitate healthy lifestyles effectively.

It is accepted that disabled people are more likely than their non-disabled peers to experience the negative attitudes of others as a major barrier to education, leisure, transport and access to public services, social contact and accessibility outside the home, all of which impact on well-being (Office for National Statistics, 2014). Organisational cultures and attitudes towards people with learning disabilities are characterised by preconceived notions of difficulty and awkwardness, exacerbated by social stigma and stereotyping. The lack of awareness, understanding and knowledge of mainstream staff hinders access and treatment for people with learning disabilities.

Brown and Guvenir (2009) interviewed parents, caregivers and the nursing staff of children with learning disabilities and found that nurses reported feeling 'apprehension' because they did not 'know what to expect', and parents recounted feeling 'helpless' and 'anxious' because the health-care staff did not know their child or their child's needs. Healthcare systems are complex and busy environments, but professionals need to ensure they consider the individual's needs and adapt existing systems to meet them. Health care workers are ideally placed to promote health, and an awareness and understanding of people with learning disabilities is essential in determining how best to communicate and promote the healthy lifestyle message.

How can we promote health for people with learning disability?

There are clear and significant health inequalities in relation to physical inactivity according to income, gender, age, ethnicity and disability (NHS, 2009). Promoting active lifestyles can help address some of the important challenges. Increasing physical activity has the potential to improve both physical and mental health, reduce all-cause mortality and improve life expectancy (DH, 2011).

It is important for practitioners to find out about a persons' interests and to be well informed about local amenities, sports clubs and activities that are available for free. Encourage exercise. Just as people with learning disabilities and those supporting them need to understand what is on offer, they need to be aware of the common health problems experienced by people with learning disabilities and the factors that can cause problems with access to health information and health care.

People with learning disabilities make up about 2% of the population, but only around a quarter are identified in GP learning disability registers and/or are known to specialist learning disability services. All people with learning disabilities aged 14 or over who are on their GP's learning disability register are entitled to an annual health check and a health action plan. In 2014/15, just under 50% of those on registers had a health check, and one way to encourage and promote health is to encourage the uptake of these. It is important to note that people with learning disabilities may not recognise early warning signs and symptoms themselves. They need to have equitable access to health checks to spot health conditions early and maintain good health. For example:

- Cancer screening – focuses on increasing the uptake of the three national screening programmes for breast, bowel and cervical cancer. While there are pockets of good practice in England, we need to spread the learning to ensure that screening levels are consistently high.

- Innovative regional pilots, for example exploring the introduction of new screening learning disability liaison nurses in the North East and Cumbria, to improve uptake.

- Flu jabs – working with Public Health England (PHE) to ensure that children and adults with learning disabilities are clearly identified as a clinically 'at risk' group that is eligible for a flu jab, as part of the annual flu programme. Accessible literature, developed by PHE, is also encouraging people to register for a flu vaccination

There are a number of simple things that can be done to achieve health benefits and here are some examples of the best approaches to use when working with people with learning disabilities. Reasonable adjustments under the Equality Act (2010) can mean alterations to the environment by providing lifts, wider doors, ramps and/or tactile signage, but may also mean changes to policies, procedures and staff training to ensure that services work equally well for all people. Raising awareness of learning disabilities is crucial in all public services. Every person should be treated with respect and dignity – remember you do not know the difficulties the people you meet are facing, whether they have a mental illness, dementia or a learning disability. As a general rule, listen, observe and check the person's understanding. Use every opportunity presented to encourage a healthy lifestyle, signpost people to support groups, provide Easy Read information, and be positive and engaging. People may require clear, simple and possibly repeated explanations of what is happening or required, and of treatments to be followed. They may need help with appointments and help with managing lifestyle changes and in understanding reasons for the necessity to change. They may need information in different formats, such as practical demonstrations, Easy Read leaflets, pictures or simplistic language. Read all information that has been provided; ask accompanying support staff for information or clarification. Family carers and staff also need to be aware that health professionals may value the information they hold about the person. Ask more questions about any communication or support needs, and check understanding and recollection of information.

What good health promotion looks like

The table below outlines ways we can support people to lead healthier lives. Use the table when considering the case studies that follow.

Objective	What you can do	Questions to ask	Follow up
To support the person with LD	Be prepared and knowledgeable. Find out about local support groups clubs, activities and health promotions. Record the person's needs and interests clearly and concisely. Always use opportunities to encourage a healthy lifestyle. Talk about what is meant by a healthy diet – different food types, ready meals, the importance of fresh vegetables and fruit, reduction in sugar intake etc). Signpost the person to others who can help, like support groups and experts. Provide information in Easy Read format if appropriate. Think about how to engage the individual in new groups.	How do they wish to be treated? What are their priorities? Do they understand the components of a healthy lifestyle? Do they wish to engage? Do they have a clear understanding of all that is involved? Where they are going? Do they know what to expect?	Review

Objective	What you can do	Questions to ask	Follow up
To support the person to access other services	Prepare a hospital passport to help others understand important personal information about them, if appropriate. Establish whether they need support to attend appointments and help in communication. Provide the rationale for procedures and explain, repeatedly if necessary. Offer the reason for why they are necessary. Provide relevant Easy Read information in the right format for the individual. Think, do they require transport? Make suitable appointment times. Raise awareness of the possible issues involved to staff involved in the individuals care. Check people have the support to access and make visits happen.	Does the individual know how to contact the GP? Do they have contact details for all medical services, i.e. dentist, GP, opticians etc? Are there systems in place to avoid appointments being missed? Do they have all information they require, and a rationale provided for visits?	Follow up and record dates and times with the outcome and date of review. Review

Objective	What you can do	Questions to ask	Follow up
Support the person to look after and improve their physical and mental well-being	Encourage the individual to eat healthily. Encourage exercise. Gather information about support groups club and recreational activities in the local area. Found out about their interests. Find which forms of exercise they most enjoy. Try to incorporate exercise into an activity the person enjoys. E.g. if they like music, encourage dancing. Offer clear explanations and rationales as to why exercise and healthy eating are important.	Does the individual understand? Have they received education and information? Does the individual understand the purpose of the exercise? Is it for work, hobbies or targets?	Review
Learning to self-manage	Educate yourself and know what to look for. Help the person to recognise warning signs for common complaints (particularly relating to syndromes). Provide access to information on their condition. Support the person to monitor their own health	Has the individual received all available information in the correct format? Have they understood? Do they know what signs and symptoms to look out for?	Writing diaries and inquiry

Case study: Philip

Philip is 43-year-old man with mild learning disabilities who was admitted to the ward last week via the accident and emergency department after he was found semi-conscious in the high street having fallen down a flight of steps. He was hyperglycaemic and had suffered a broken tibia in his fall.

Philip is due to be discharged home in five days' time. He will be going home with a leg in a plaster cast that goes from just below his knee to the tips of his toes. Philip has been diagnosed with Type 2 diabetes and is clinically obese. He has given an appointment with the dietician for the following week. He is still finding his leg painful and is taking regular analgesics.

Considering Philip's case, what health promotion needs should be discussed before he is discharged?

Case study: Stanley

Stanley is 60 years old and has lived all his life in a large institutional setting. He has a moderate learning disability and a limited vocabulary. He has recently moved into a supported living flat. His best friend lives next door. Stanley's hobby is horse riding, which he loves.

Since moving into his flat he has put on a stone in three weeks. This is a common issue that is often overlooked. What might the reasons be for his weight gain in this situation and what support could be put in place to help him?

Case study: Miss Callis

Miss Callis is 68 years old and has a mild learning disability. She moved from Cyprus to England 40 years ago with her family and lives in a terraced house in London. Her parents passed away two years ago and her brother died a year ago. Her niece, Maria, works full time and visits at weekends.

Miss Callis has osteoarthritis (OA) affecting both her hip joints, and Type 2 diabetes. Over the last five years she has experienced increased pain, stiffness and reduced range of movement. She recently fell while hanging out her washing. She experiences pain when climbing the stairs to reach the toilet and as a result she has reduced her fluid intake. She had a urinary tract infection and her diabetes is no longer within the recommended guidelines. She takes medication for her OA and diabetes.

Miss Callis sleeps poorly, has lost her appetite and has lost a lot of weight. She is finding it difficult to carry out the personal and domestic activities of daily living. She is tearful and has stopped visiting friends. Maria has recently been doing more of the household duties and getting the shopping. She feels very tired and is finding it difficult to cope.

What could be done to promote the health and well-being of Miss Callis in relation to her physical health, her mental health, and her social care needs?

Key learning points

Good practice in health promotion is inherent not only in ensuring that each individual receives regular health checks but also revolves around taking advantage of each opportunity to offer advice and guidance. Help people understand for themselves the signs and symptoms to look out for. Encourage a healthy lifestyle in terms of healthy diet and exercise and offer a good rationale as to why this is advantageous. Be knowledgeable and help others understand what is meant by healthy diet. Ensure that the person has fully understood any procedures or information given. Be able to provide information in a suitable format about local support groups and activities that can help support an individual. Nurture an ability to be flexible and creative in your approach bearing in mind to always be respectful of each person. Barriers to health promotion for people with learning disabilities are not insurmountable and can often be overcome by minor adjustment to practice, attitude, education and awareness. Successfully promote good physical and mental health by being alert to opportunities. Act as a role model. Be positive in your approach. Think forward and ensure the person receives the support, advice and guidance they need.

References

Brown FJ & Guvenir J (2009) The experiences of children with learning disabilities, their carers and staff during a hospital admission. *British Journal of Learning Disabilities* **37** 110–115. doi:10.1111 /j.1468-3156.2008.00522.

Cairns G, Angus K, Hastings G & Caraher M (2013) Systematic reviews of the evidence on the nature, extent and effects of food marketing to children. A retrospective summary. *Appetite* **62** 209–215.

Department of Health (2001) *Valuing People, a new strategy for learning disability for the 21st century: a white paper.*

Department of Health (2011) *Physical Activity, Health Improvement and Protection Start Active, Stay Active.*

Department of Health (2013) *Confidential Inquiry into Premature Deaths of People with Learning Disabilities.*

Disability Rights Commission (2006) *Equal Treatment: Closing the gap*. Leeds: Disability Rights Commission.

Emerson E, Glover G, Turner S, Greig R, Hatton C, Baines S, Copeland A, Evison F, Roberts H, Robertson J & Welch V (2012) Improving health and lives: The Learning Disabilities Public Health Observatory. *Advances in Mental Health and Intellectual Disabilities* **6** 26-32 10.1108/20441281211198835.

Marmot M (2010) Fair Society, Healthy Lives: the Marmot Review [online]. Available at: "http://www.parliament.uk/documents/fair-society-healthy-lives-full-report.pdf" www.parliament.uk/documents/fair-society-healthy-lives-full-report.pdf (accessed February 2018).

Mencap (2007) *Death by Indifference*. London: Mencap.

Mencap (2012) *Death by indifference: 74 deaths and counting. A progress report 5 years on*. London: Mencap.

Michael (2008) *Healthcare for All: Independent inquiry into access to healthcare for people with learning disabilities*. London: Aldrick press.

NHS (2009) *Health Survey for England 2008: Physical activity and fitness*. London: NHS Information Centre for Health and Social Care.

Office for National Statistics (2014) Life Opportunities Survey: Understanding disability wave two, part II [online]. Available at: https://www.gov.uk/government/statistics/life-opportunities-survey-wave-2-part-2-results (accessed December 2017).

Public Health England (2015) *Inequalities in health and life expectancies persist in England and its local authority areas*. London: PHE.

The Marmot Review: www.instituteofhealthequity.org/projects/fair-society-healthy-lives-the-marmot-review

World Health Organization (2005) *Noncommunicable disease and poverty* [online]. Available at: http://www.wpro.who.int/publications/docs/poverty_ncd.pdf (accessed December 2017).

Chapter 7:

Physical health

By Peter Woodward

Aims

This chapter aims to introduce some of the reasons that people with learning disabilities are more likely to become unwell and look at some of the illnesses they are likely to develop. It describes some of the difficulties involved in assessing people with learning disabilities and ways to overcome them. It provides advice on how to support people with learning disabilities to access and use health services.

This chapter does not cover health promotion, which has been discussed in chapter 6. Issues around capacity and consent form a large part of meeting an individual's health needs, and these concepts are covered further in Section 4: Staying safe.

Summary

People with learning disabilities are more likely to become unwell than members of the public as a whole, and they will have a shorter lifespan (Emerson & Baines, 2010). They may also develop a different set of health problems than could be expected in the general population (Hardy *et al*, 2013). When people with learning disabilities become unwell it can be difficult to identify that something is wrong. This can be made worse by communication barriers and health services not adjusting to the individual's needs. There are ways to overcome this, such as being aware of certain health problems, adapting methods of communication and providing the individual with additional support.

Why are people with learning disabilities more likely to have health problems?

People with learning disabilities are, as a whole, more likely to become unwell than the general population. However, it is important to understand that the reasons why people with mild learning disabilities become unwell can differ from why people with more severe and profound learning disabilities become unwell. While those with mild learning disabilities tend to develop health problems due to a lack of understanding or inadequate education about healthy living, people with more severe learning disabilities often present with a different profile of illness due to having genetic syndromes, like cerebral palsy, Down's syndrome or brain damage, for example, which may predispose them to certain health conditions.

A good example of the problem of the lack of education for adults with mild learning disabilities is that they are more likely to be overweight (Marshall *et al*, 2003; Harris *et al*, 2003; Emerson, 2005). The reasons for gaining weight are the same for all people, whether they have learning disabilities or not, and people with mild learning disabilities who live independently or semi-independently will often prepare meals themselves, which are often convenience foods or take-away foods high in calories. Added to this, and often causing it, is that people with learning disabilities may not understand complicated diets or information on weight loss/gain, and important concepts such as calories, protein, fibre, fats and carbohydrates may not have been explained to them in a way that they understand.

In addition to this, people with learning disabilities tend to be less active, play less sport and do not have leisure or work activities, all of which means they burn fewer calories, and some medications that are more likely to be prescribed to people with learning disabilities can cause weight gain in the long term.

Several factors therefore combine to cause people with mild learning disabilities to gain weight. Once overweight, they are more prone to developing heart disease, diabetes and many other weight-related health problems.

Individuals with more severe learning disabilities may encounter different illnesses. An example of this is gastro oesophageal reflux disease (GORD), which is often due to low muscle tone preventing the stomach being held shut once food enters it, allowing it to travel back up the oesophagus. People with severe or profound learning disabilities are also more likely to be on medication with side effects, have physical disabilities, poorer immune systems, and be genetically predisposed to illnesses.

Health conditions that may be seen in higher levels in people with learning disabilities:

- **Obesity** and all the health problems associated with it (note that people with profound learning disabilities are often underweight).

- **Respiratory problems** such as asthma, chest infections and serious conditions such as pneumonia, which could be caused by food or drink entering the lungs.

- **GORD**, which can lead to a damaged oesophagus and possibly even cancer of the oesophagus.

- **Dental/oral health** is more like to be problematic for people with learning disabilities and they are more likely to have reactive dental work to fix problems than work to prevent problems occurring. Some medications can also affect gums or give the individual a dry mouth.

- **Sight, vision and hearing problems** are more likely in people with learning disabilities and will increase with more severe learning disabilities and with some genetic syndromes. People with learning disabilities may require additional support in eye or hearing examinations and may need prompting to use their glasses and hearing aids.

- **Diabetes** is seen in higher levels in people with learning disabilities, often for the same reasons that obesity is.

- **Epilepsy** is much more common in people with learning disabilities. Epilepsy is associated with damage to the brain so the more severe the learning disability the more likely epilepsy is to occur.

- **Swallowing problems** are more common in people with learning disabilities. They become more prevalent in people with severe and profound learning disabilities and in some syndromes. They can cause serious complications, especially if food and drink enters the lungs. Some people may have to be fed through a tube (called a a percutaneous endoscopic gastrostomy (PEG)) in to the stomach if their swallowing problems are very severe.

- **Mobility problems** are associated with some syndromes and increase with the severity of learning disabilities. These can range from problems with co-ordination to individuals requiring wheelchairs and hoists.

- **Heart problems** are more likely in people with learning disabilities for two reasons. An individual may be born with heart problems such as those seen in people with Down's syndrome, or heart disease can be developed due to having an inactive lifestyle and a poor diet.

- **Hypothyroidism** is associated with Down's syndrome.

- **Sexual health** can be an issue for people with learning disabilities. When people with learning disabilities are sexually active they can be vulnerable.

- **Helicobacter pylori** is a bacteria that can live in the stomach. It can cause stomach ulcers that are thought to increase the likelihood of stomach cancer. Helicobacter pylori is much more likely to be found in the stomachs of people with learning disabilities, particularly in people with more severe learning disabilities and those who live or attend day centres with other people with learning disabilities. Re-infection is common.

- **Constipation** can be a serious problem for people with learning disabilities. Often there is an over reliance on laxatives rather than encouraging a diet high in fibre, staying hydrated and encouraging exercise.

- **Infections** of the chest or urinary tract are more common among people with learning disabilities.

- **Cancer** affects people with learning disabilities as much as the general population, however there are some differences in the types of cancers seen. They may, for example, develop cancers that are not seen as much in people without learning disabilities, including: oesophageal cancer (associated with GORD) and stomach cancer (associated with helicobacter pylori). Some genetic syndromes are associated with particular cancers, for example men with Down's syndrome are more likely to have cancer of the genitals. At the same time, people with learning disabilities are less likely to develop lung cancer because smoking is not as common, and there are lower levels of skin cancer if there is less exposure to harmful UV rays. Cervical cancer will be also lower if an individual is not sexually active, meaning they are not exposed to the human papilloma virus that causes cervical cancer.

- **Specific syndromes** are associated with specific health problems. Down's syndrome, for example, is associated with heart problems, diabetes, high blood pressure, sight and hearing problems, epilepsy, respiratory conditions, sleep problems, dental issues, thyroid disorder and problems with muscles joints and bones, to name a few. Information about specific syndromes is freely available on the internet. If an individual has a syndrome, support workers, family members or carers should find out if there is any associated health problem to look out for.

Problems accessing healthcare

Although people with learning disabilities have higher levels of health needs, there are often problems when they do access healthcare. This can be for a range of different reasons.

■ There may be difficulties physically accessing health services. This may be due to distance, expense, or needing additional support.

■ People with learning disabilities may not know that a service exists, such as a drop-in clinic. Finding out about services may be difficult if the internet or telephone are needed to book appointments.

■ People with learning disabilities may not be offered the same screening opportunities. For example, cervical screening may not be offered if the individual is assumed not to be sexually active.

■ There is often confusion around consent laws. Most people with learning disabilities should have the capacity to make decisions regarding their treatment. When an individual lacks capacity, decisions should be made in their best interests.

■ People with learning disabilities may not be offered surgery or a medical procedure if it is felt that they would not concord with the procedure or the rehabilitation following it.

■ A lot of resources may not be aimed at conditions people with learning disabilities can contract. For example, the government's priorities are reducing levels of skin, lung and bowel cancer, which are more common in the population at large, whereas oesophageal cancer and stomach cancer are more common in people with learning disabilities.

Identifying and recognising the signs and symptoms of illness

Assessing for health problems involves looking for signs and symptoms of the illness. Signs are the visible indicators that the person is unwell, such as swelling, bruising, discoloration, bleeding or examining an X-Ray. Symptoms are the feelings and sensations the individual is experiencing, such as dizziness, confusion and itching, as well as pain, in its many forms.

Some typical indicators that someone could be unwell include:

Bad breath	Vomiting	Drinking more fluids	Absences or looking vacant
Grimacing or appearing to be in pain	Sweating	Straining to breath	Constipation
Feinting	Weeping or crying	Gaining weight or losing weight	Coughs
Rubbing or scratching parts of the body	Sneezing	Vomiting	Limping
Diarrhoea	A very high temperature	Shivering	Low appetite or avoiding food
Swelling	Discoloured or smelly urine	Belching/burping	Loss of appetite
Bleeding (e.g. gums, piles, blood in stools)	Yellowing of skin or the whites of eyes	Choking	Dark or light coloured stools

Usually when someone is unwell the obvious thing to do is to ask them how they feel, about levels of discomfort or other symptoms. Unfortunately, when an individual has problems with communicating there is a greater reliance on looking for signs of illness. This is a lot more difficult to do if someone with learning disabilities shows their discomfort in different ways. The more severe the learning disabilities are, the more there is a reliance on observing them for signs and symptoms.

As well as these 'signs' there may be behaviours that are not typical of illness. If someone has never had challenging behaviour before, for example, but they start displaying challenging behaviours or their challenging behaviours suddenly start to increase, this could be a sign of illness. Challenging behaviours are usually due to an individual's environment but on some occasions may indicate being unwell. For example, self-injury that is dedicated to a particular part of the body such as poking or hitting the ear may indicate earache. Hitting the side of the mouth make indicate dental pain. Pushing fingers into orifices such as the anus could be due to constipation or excessive scratching due to haemorrhoids (piles). Some of other indicators include:

- sucking of the hand, which has been associated with reflux

- screaming or loud vocalisations, which could indicate pain

- incontinence such as wetting the bed when an individual does not normally do this could be an indicator of a urinary tract infection

- refusing to get out of bed, withdrawing or refusing to do activities that they normally enjoy can all indicate that there is a health problem.

Behaviours like incontinence or self-injury are more common in people with more severe learning disabilities, and because of this they can be overlooked. This is called 'diagnostic overshadowing', where the behaviour that could indicate pain or discomfort is attributed to the learning disabilities rather than an additional illness.

Case study: Mary

Mary has severe learning disabilities and very little speech, and she lives in a house with other people with severe learning disabilities. In Mary's house there have been a number of staff changes recently. This happened at a time when Mary's health started to deteriorate. Over a few months, Mary went from being continent to wetting the bed five times a night. Staff have noticed, but because of the number of staff changes they do not know that this is unusual for Mary. Some of the other men and women living with Mary also have night time incontinence and the staff team think it is a normal behaviour for people living there. The incontinence becomes associated with Mary's disability rather than a new medical condition that can be treated.

This case shows how a member of staff who has worked with someone for a long time will know an individual well. They can identify changes that are different. Anyone new to this individual, such as a new health professional or support worker will not have the same knowledge and would not recognise deterioration over a long period. This is why records can be important – they demonstrate changes to how someone is presenting now and how they were in the past.

'I was assessing a young lady with severe learning disabilities and asked the member of staff supporting her how long she has been pulling at her ear. The member of staff could not answer as she worked for an agency and had only been employed for two days.'
A doctor

Screening and tests

There are times when people with learning disabilities, as in the wider population, will need to have tests or investigations for a health problem. They should attend at least as many health check-ups as anyone else, and they may require additional tests as well.

Additional tests may be needed if:

■ the individual has a syndrome that is associated with a particular health problem

■ they are on medication that has side effects that need to be monitored

■ they have a family history of a particular health problem.

The frequency of tests will depend on the individual and their condition. For example, an individual with diabetes may require daily blood sugar monitoring. Eye tests usually take place every two years but an individual with glaucoma or a child with glasses would have more frequent eye tests. Because of this, the list below may vary per individual.

■ **Annual health checks:** All people with moderate, severe and profound learning disabilities above the age of 14 should be offered an annual health check through their GP. Some people with mild learning disabilities may also be offered annual health checks if they have complex health needs. This is tailored to their individual needs but would normally include a physical assessment checking for blood pressure, pulse, BMI and relevant blood and urine tests. The GP will monitor chronic conditions such as epilepsy, asthma or diabetes. If the individual has a genetic syndrome associated with health problems, these may be examined with greater scrutiny.

■ **Hearing tests:** The GP can examine for obvious problems such as a build-up of ear wax. If a hearing test is required, the GP will request this as a referral and an individual may require regular tests from this point on.

■ **Sight tests:** These are usually carried out every two years. However, some medical conditions such as glaucoma or diabetes or in individuals with deteriorating sight and those that are younger or older may require more regular eye tests.

■ **Dental check-ups:** Advice on the frequency of dental check-ups varies. A dentist will decide how frequently, based on an individual's needs, which may be as often as every three months. Regular visits to a hygienist for deeper cleaning may be necessary too.

- **Blood pressure:** If not an issue, blood pressure is usually checked every five years, and more regularly with age. For someone with learning disabilities, this should be part of their annual health check.

- **Helicobacter pylori:** This is not currently screened for but it is known that helicobacter pylori is more common in people with learning disabilities, particularly in people with more severe learning disabilities. Due to re-infection, it can be good practice to regularly screen for this when other blood tests take place.

- **Hepatitis B:** This is not routinely screened for but people with learning disabilities historically have been more likely to contract hepatitis B, especially people with Down's syndrome.

- **Cholesterol:** This may be tested in people who are older or prone to heart disease.

- **Thyroid function tests:** Will be regularly undertaken in people with an overactive or underactive thyroid. It is more common in people with Down's syndrome so may be regularly screened for.

- **Type 2 diabetes:** Is more common in people who are overweight and inactive. Some ethnic populations may be more at risk. A GP may want to test for this if an individual is at risk or showing symptoms of diabetes. When someone has diabetes, they may take medication and will require regular tests, and daily monitoring may be necessary.

Gender/cultural/age specific tests include:

- Breast screening begins around the age of 50 and continues every three years. Women with learning disabilities should be encouraged to self-examine their breasts.

- Cervical screening tests occur every three years in adults, increasing to five years in the over 50s.

- Testicular cancer is more common in men with Down's syndrome and they should be encouraged to examine their testicles. Staff may be able to observe lumps if assisting individuals with more severe learning disabilities with personal hygiene.

- There may be some tests which are culturally significant such as sickle cell anaemia or diabetes.

- Everybody over the age of 40 should be offered an NHS health check which should occur every five years from then on.

Having blood tests or assessments

People with learning disabilities, like many people, may not like hospitals, injections and blood tests. This can cause them anxiety. There are ways to decrease anxiety such as desensitising the individual to the environment or the procedure that they may require. There are materials available to help with this listed in the Further resources section (p211).

If someone needs to have a blood test it is worth asking if other tests can be taken from the same sample. For example, an individual having a liver function test due to being on medication may, at the same time, be tested for helicobacter pylori infection too. If someone requires an operation that requires a general anaesthetic and the individual also needs dental work, an enquiry can be made to see if it is possible to combine the two. This will cut down the risk of repeated use of general anaesthetic and avoid the need for two separate procedures. It may not always be appropriate, but if it is possible it can reduce distress and risk.

Visiting and using health services

An individual will undoubtedly have to use health services at some point in their life. The advice below will vary depending on whether the individual is in a state of emergency or not.

What to do at appointments

- First, it should be considered whether the individual needs an appointment or whether a pharmacy or NHS Direct may be able to provide appropriate advice.
- Consider whether the individual will benefit from an appointment early or a late in the day.
- Would the individual have problems with a waiting room? If so, can the first appointment of the day or straight after lunch be booked so they do not have to wait?
- Distractions may help, such as bringing books, snacks or headphones to play music. If the individual has any personal communication aids these should be brought too.
- If a longer appointment time is needed, a double appointment could be booked.
- The individual will need to know what will happen in advance of their appointment. They should be allowed to discuss what questions they may get asked or what the procedure involves. Pictures or videos (from the internet) can be used if they are available.

■ The individual needs to know about confidentiality and that anything they say to the doctor will be private.

■ It can help if the same member(s) of staff accompany the individual to follow up appointments so they are aware of what happened before. Staff may need to make notes to feedback to the rest of the team.

■ It can assist the GP if additional information can be provided. For example, how often the individual has used medications, how many bowel movements they might have had or changes in weight/sleep pattern and so on. Staff should only record what is appropriate for that condition and consent must be considered too. For example, sometimes video recordings can help identify if someone is having seizure but this will require consent or be in the individual's best interests.

■ Sometimes PRN medication like lorazepam is used to help very anxious individuals to cope. It should be noted, however, that sometimes these can interfere with diagnosis, such as when running tests for epilepsy. If this is an issue, alternative, one-off medications may be prescribed.

■ Professionals from the community learning disabilities team may be able to assist too.

■ Mencap has a section for healthcare professionals to give them advice: http://www.mencap.org.uk/all-about-learning-disability/information-professionals/health

Case study: Robert

Robert is a 21-year-old man with severe learning disabilities and challenging behaviour. He lives at home with his parents. Robert's gums have started bleeding and his parents want his dentist to examine him. Robert also has epilepsy and can have clusters of night time seizures where he wakes feeling tired and irritable. Robert does not like crowds and noise and the last time he visited the GP he started to bite his hand because he found sitting in the waiting room for 15 minutes stressful.

Robert's parents looked at possible solutions to make Robert's dental appointment as successful as possible.

They contacted the dentist and requested the first appointment after lunch at a specific time so that there would not be a wait. This avoids mornings, which can be more challenging. They spoke to the dentist before the appointment and discussed the best ways of communicating with Robert, what he likes and what he gets uncomfortable with. They left copies of some of the pages of his hospital passport which they thought would help. They requested an extended appointment so that any corrective work could be carried out after the check up without having to make a second appointment. The day before the appointment they took Robert to the dentist's surgery to show him the waiting room so that it was less of a shock the next day. They also took photographs to show him the next day before setting off.

On the day of the appointment, they took along some of Robert's favourite activities – a colouring book, a portable DVD player with his headphones, a stress ball, a handheld video game and a bottle of sparkling water, which he likes. They also took a communication board that Robert uses to help make his needs known and anything else that they thought might help the dentist, such as Robert's toothbrush, the toothpaste he prefers and a list of the medications he is on.

The dentist was able to identify that Robert has gingivitis. He also got Robert to clean his teeth and said that Robert was not cleaning the teeth at the back of his mouth and cleaning the teeth at the front too vigorously. The dentist recommended a new toothpaste and using a different kind of brush. He recommended Robert use a timer so that he brushes his teeth evenly for two minutes.

Following an appointment

People with learning disabilities may require additional support following an appointment with health services. They may need to be supported at the pharmacy, told the side effects of medications and be reminded to take medications. Pharmacists may give medication in dosset boxes, which have separate compartments to put the medicines in for each day of the week and times of the day such as morning, afternoon, evening and night. There are also free applications that work on smart phones or electronic tablets that can serve as a reminder to take medication, or setting a daily alarm or phoning at specific times can assist with this.

'I went to the doctor and was prescribed Fluoxetine, but when I got to the pharmacist they gave me something called Prozac. I was confused but my support worker explained they were the same thing.'
Expert by Experience, Jo, who has mild learning disabilities

When medication is prescribed, a doctor may need to be told about swallowing problems or difficulty with tablets so that liquid medications can be prescribed. Side effects may need to be explained in a way that can be clearly understood. If medications can take some time to start working, this needs to be explained too.

'I supported a man who would suck the coating off his tablets which tasted sweet and would then spit it out when he got through to the actual, bitter tasting, medication. Another man used to crunch through his slow-release epilepsy tablets instead of swallowing them. He would get a sudden high dose, followed by a sub-therapeutic dose instead of an even dose of medication across the day.'
Learning disabilities nurse

Hospital passports

Some people with learning disabilities have accompanying information that they can take with them if they need to access health services. These may go under various names, such as 'health passports', 'patient's passport' or 'hospital book'. They usually include the individual's medical history, current medications, allergies, diagnosis and other important information that can help health professionals. It also gives advice on methods of communication, likes and dislikes, cultural issues, religious wishes and other important information.

The NHS has a free downloadable template which can easily be found online with an internet search.

Reasonable adjustments

Public sector heath service providers are required by law to make 'reasonable adjustments' for people with learning disabilities. These adjustments should remove barriers that prevent people with learning disabilities accessing health services. Most may think of making adjustments such as adding ramps to allow wheelchair access, however there are far more than just physical barriers.

If they are required, people with learning disabilities:

- should be provided with information in an accessible way

- should be provided with specific times for appointments

- should have their wishes taken into consideration such as listed in a 'hospital passport'

- should be offered annual health checks and proactively seek to identify unidentified health needs

- should be identified by health services who should take their additional needs in to consideration. Ideally these should be electronic alerts so that reasonable adjustments can be made.

- Should receive assistance from community learning disabilities teams or learning disabilities liaison workers should be sought.

Key learning points

- People with learning disabilities are more likely to develop all the illnesses seen in the population as a whole.

- People with learning disabilities may also develop some illnesses that are less common in the general population.

- Even although people with learning disabilities are more likely to be unwell, they receive worse treatment.

There are ways to help:

- Be aware of and identify the types of illness someone may contract.

- Identify the signs and symptoms of these illnesses.

- Support an individual to communicate their needs.

- Help them to access health services and hold those services accountable.

- Ensure that regular health checks take place.

- Health services need to make reasonable adjustments to ensure that people with learning disabilities' needs are met.

References

Emerson E & Baines S (2010) Health inequalities & people with learning disabilities in the UK [online]. *Tizard Learning Disability Review* **16** (1). Available at: http://www.complexneeds.org.uk/ modules/Module-4.1-Working-with-other-professionals/All/downloads/m13p020c/emerson_baines_ health_inequalities.pdf (accessed December 2017)

Hardy S, Woodward P, Woolard P & Tait T (2013) *Meeting the Health Needs of People with Learning Disabilities: RCN guidance*. London: Royal College of Nursing.

Hardy S, Chaplin E & Woodward P (2010) *Mental health nursing of adults with learning disabilities: RCN guidance*. London: Royal College of Nursing.

Further resources

www.easyhealth.org.uk/

www.mencap.org.uk/advice-and-support/health

Chapter 8:

Mental health

By Karina Marshall-Tate and Eddie Chaplin

Aims

- To understand mental health and how to promote mental well-being.
- To recognise symptoms of poor mental health and how this can present in people with learning disabilities.
- To understand common mental illnesses.
- To understand the support needs of people with common mental illnesses.

Summary

Mental health and physical health are linked and dependant on each other. Mental health, like physical health, is therefore essential to our well-being. This chapter introduces mental health and how we can spot common mental illnesses. It also aims to show how we can support people with a learning disability to achieve good mental health.

Introduction

In this chapter, we will explore what mental health is, why it is important for people with a learning disability, and the role that support staff and/or family carers can play in supporting individuals to maintain their mental health and well-being. Finally, we will look at some of the warning signs that could indicate that someone is experiencing mental health difficulties, what we can do to support that person, and how to get help.

What is mental health?

Mental health, or mental well-being, is a state of health that enables us to live fulfilled lives and cope with everyday stressors. It is not merely about the absence of mental illness, but about our whole being.

We all have mental health and we can all experience periods of mental ill health. This can be in relation to life events, such as loss and bereavement, stress or relationship difficulties, or there can be no identifiable cause. Some mental health difficulties can be linked to specific episodes of mental illness such as depression or psychosis. In all cases, the way that people experience mental health and mental illness is different and it can vary over their lifespan. For example, a person with schizophrenia will be able to lead an ordinary life when they are mentally well but may require periods of health care while unwell.

People with learning disabilities, like the wider population, can experience periods of mental health difficulties or mental ill health. However, it is only over the last 30 years that health staff have acknowledged this and it is only recently that mental health and well-being for people with a learning disability as well as the wider population has been recognised as a significant factor in public health, health service planning and delivery.

Mental health and well-being

There has been a significant shift in attitudes toward mental health recently. The Duke and Duchess of Cambridge, and Prince Harry, are actively promoting mental health to combat stigma and encourage open dialogue about mental health issues through their 'Heads Together' campaign[2]. The government has publicly committed to removing injustices in mental health care and improving mental health services in the NHS (HM Government, 2017), and many celebrities have spoken openly about their mental health difficulties. The NHS has promoted mental health and well-being with the 'Five Ways to Wellbeing' initiative (HM Government, 2008). The research that underpinned this initiative found that small changes to our daily lives can have a significant impact on our mental health and well-being and help people to flourish.

Breaking down stigma and promoting mental health will have huge benefits and *must* be inclusive of people with learning disabilities.

---

2   For more information, visit www.headstogether.org.uk

The 'Five Ways to Wellbeing' are:

Connect...	With the people around you. With family, friends, colleagues and neighbours. At home, work, school or in your local community. Think of these as the cornerstones of your life and invest time in developing them. Building these connections will support and enrich you every day.
Be active...	Go for a walk or run. Step outside. Cycle. Play a game. Garden. Dance. Exercising makes you feel good. Most importantly, discover a physical activity you enjoy and that suits your level of mobility and fitness.
Take notice...	Be curious. Catch sight of the beautiful. Remark on the unusual. Notice the changing seasons. Savour the moment, whether you are walking to work, eating lunch or talking to friends. Be aware of the world around you and what you are feeling. Reflecting on your experiences will help you appreciate what matters to you.
Keep learning...	Try something new. Rediscover an old interest. Sign up for that course. Take on a different responsibility at work. Fix a bike. Learn to play an instrument or how to cook your favourite food. Set a challenge you will enjoy achieving. Learning new things will make you more confident as well as being fun.
Give...	Do something nice for a friend, or a stranger. Thank someone. Smile. Volunteer your time. Join a community group. Look out, as well as in. Seeing yourself, and your happiness, linked to the wider community can be incredibly rewarding and creates connections with the people around you.

(HM Government, 2008)

These five ways are no different for people with learning disabilities, however carers and/or family members may have to support an individual to achieve them as some people with a learning disability can experience significant barriers in trying achieving them. Historically, social exclusion and institutionalisation prevented access to such initiatives, and latterly, community access and community participation remains a challenge for some people with a learning disability and their family and carers. Contemporary approaches to care and support such as active support, person centred care and positive behaviour support can work in parallel with the Five Ways to Wellbeing, and indeed they share common themes. By incorporating the Five Ways into care and support practices, support workers, carers and family carers can help to promote the mental health and well-being of people with a learning disability. These do not have to be grand gestures, such as volunteering, but can be simple things that can be achieved daily, like taking time to notice the world around us or smiling and saying good morning to our neighbours as a way of connecting with others.

Case study: Supporting mental health with the Five Ways to Wellbeing

Akinwale lives in supported accommodation with three other men and a team of support workers. He had a good relationship with Kevin, the area manager, and they enjoy playing football and computer games together. Unfortunately, Kevin was transferred to a new location and Akinwale was no longer able to see him. After a couple of weeks, the remaining staff and Akinwale's housemates noticed that he was more quiet than usual and that, although he still participated in activities with them, he did not seem as interested or to be enjoying them as much. Akinwale told them that he missed Kevin and felt sad and lonely. The staff and housemates decided to use the Five Ways to support Akinwale while he experienced these mental health difficulties. They supported him to connect with Kevin by sending him a postcard; they helped him to be more active by encouraging him to try new activities; and they helped him by showing his housemates how to play the computer games that he used to play with Kevin. Gradually, Akinwale began to return to his normal self and was able to adjust to his new circumstances.

The mental health needs of people with a learning disability

People with a learning disability can experience higher rates of mental health difficulties and mental illness than the wider population. The reasons for this are varied and complex but can be broadly categorised in three ways: predisposing, precipitating and perpetuating factors. That is, factors that make people more vulnerable to developing a mental illness, factors that trigger a mental illness, and factors that maintain or exacerbate mental health difficulties. These factors can be broken down further into biological, psychological and social vulnerabilities (see Table 1). Life events, such as bereavement, bullying, stress and problems at work, can also affect our mental health.

Predisposing factors to poor mental health

Biological	Genetic syndromes such as Prader-Willi, Lesch Nyhan or DiGeorge
	Epilepsy
	Some medications
	Brain damage
	Physical health conditions
Psychological	Poor problem solving or coping skills
	Difficulties recognising and communicating thoughts, feelings and distress
Social	Isolation
	Social exclusion
	Deprivation
	Unemployment
	Poor housing

(Adapted from Chaplin *et al*, 2016)

People with a learning disability are more likely to experience these precipitating, predisposing and perpetuating factors than the wider population, and therefore have higher rates of mental illness. When a person with a learning disability experiences mental health difficulties they are also more likely to be hospitalised out of area – that is, far from their home and family and carers – and they are more likely to be prescribed higher rates of psychotropic medications (medicines to treat mental illnesses). These medications can help people experiencing mental illnesses such as schizophrenia, bipolar disorder or severe depression, however they have also been prescribed as a way to 'manage' challenging behaviour in the absence of a mental illness in people with a learning disability[3].

However, there is no evidence of their efficacy in treating challenging behaviour, although their short-term use to manage an acute episode of violent or dangerous behaviour is commonly accepted practice. In some cases, medication can also have debilitating side effects for some people and so the prescription of such medicines

---

3   For more information, see the NHS STOMP campaign: https://www.england.nhs.uk/learning-disabilities/improving-health/stomp/

needs to be made after careful and extensive assessment by an experienced clinician (RCP, 2016).

Mental health promotion and mental well-being should therefore be a significant factor in care and support plans to promote resilience and coping strategies, to reduce the impact of potential stressors, and to reduce a person's vulnerability to developing mental health difficulties.

Recognising and responding to concerns about mental health

When our mental health and well-being is vulnerable, we may see changes in the way that we think, act and do things. For example, we may interpret things in negative ways, we may change our behaviour by not doing things that we used to, or by doing new things to try and block out difficult feelings – like using illicit drugs or alcohol – or our motivation to do things may change. Other signs that someone may be experiencing mental health difficulties include:

- Changes in sleep pattern.
- Changes in appetite.
- Withdrawal and self-isolation.
- Increased use of alcohol or drugs.
- Headaches, neck and shoulder aches.
- Changes in mood – irritability, sadness.
- Tearfulness.
- Loss of interest in activities/hobbies.

Recognising these mental health difficulties and talking with friends and family or paid carers/support workers can often help to resolve them, particularly when steps are taken to promote mental well-being using the Five Ways or similar approaches.

Case study: supporting mental well-being – Joe's day service

Joe has a learning disability and attends his local day service three days a week. He has friends there and enjoys the activities, but mostly the company of others. The service is closing as part of a redesign and Joe is very worried about this as he does not yet have an alternative service. His care staff recognise that he is anxious as he paces around repeating 'closure' and cries. They know that he has experienced mental health difficulties in the past and they want to minimise the risk of this happening to Joe again. Joe and his team talk about their concerns and decide to be proactive in minimising the disruption. Joe is supported to buy an address book and record the names and addresses of his friends and their carers so that they can keep in contact. They arrange a meeting all together to discuss the closure and agree that once a week they will meet to go bowling and have a meal at the local leisure centre. Joe remains worried about the closure but he has stopped pacing and crying because he can still be active, connect, and learn new things as part of the group initiative.

Role of the support worker/family carers

Support workers can be instrumental in helping a person with a learning disability to recognise and communicate their feelings and then work in partnership to find ways to improve mental well-being. When supporting someone with a mental health difficulty it is important to listen and give the person time and space to express themselves. Some people with a learning disability may not be able to verbally communicate their thoughts and feelings, and could instead show their distress through behaviour that challenges us. Non-judgemental, person-centred approaches that are tailored to the person's communication needs should form the basis of any care and support. Practical steps that may help to reduce distress could be:

- Show the person that they are valued.
- Give the person opportunities to make choices.
- Find relaxing activities i.e. music, adult colouring, walking.
- Temporarily provide relief from stressful situations i.e. a 'duvet day', skipping chores, having a lie in.
- Provide temporary extra support to increase participation in activities.
- Increase time with family or friends or keyworkers.

With support from friends and family these mental health difficulties are likely to resolve themselves, however for some people this will not be the case. The mental health difficulties may become more pronounced and overwhelming. They may impact on the person's ability to go about their daily lives. When this happens, then support should be sought from health services.

Getting help

Case study: Joe's deteriorating mental health

Joe's day service eventually closed and he still did not have an alternative service to go to. While he and his group of friends continued to meet, some had left the group and sometimes the group would be cancelled at short notice. He spent most of his time in the house by himself. Joe's staff team began to notice that he was becoming anxious again. Joe was pacing and crying and did not want to eat with the others and he was not sleeping well. The staff noticed that Joe had lost weight as his clothes were very baggy and he was becoming irritable, shouting and slamming doors. They supported Joe to see his GP who was concerned that he was showing signs of depression. The GP referred Joe to his mental health in learning disability team for assessment and treatment.

When a person's mental health difficulties affects their day-to-day life and ability to carry out their normal routines, then the first place to seek support is usually through the GP. GPs can assess mental health difficulties, make referrals to mental health services where appropriate or can treat mild mental health problems within the surgery e.g. prescribe medication or talking therapy. It is important to alert the GP that the person has a learning disability and may therefore require reasonable adjustments during the consultation (reasonable adjustments are a legal obligation to all public services to make physical and psycho-social adjustments to their services to allow equal access for people with disabilities). The GP will require information about the nature of the problem, how long it has been going on for, what changes have occurred and what the concerns are from the perspective of the person with a learning disability and from any staff or family carers who may be involved. It is helpful to take along any medications that the person may be taking as well as any communication aids or items that may help the person with the consultation.

Examples of mental health difficulties that require healthcare intervention include:

- Feelings of lethargy, lacking energy and motivation.
- Thoughts become negative and the person may feel their situation is helpless.
- Problems concentrating.
- Eating too much or too little, with changes to their weight/appearance.
- Sleeping too much or too little.

- Getting easily emotional or tense and experiencing mood swings. They may also be in a state where they are constantly worried, nervous or scared. This may cause conflict in everyday situations.

- Physical symptoms might include racing pulse, feeling sick, feeling that there is something physically wrong with them.

- Unpleasant thoughts that they can't stop thinking about and which cause them stress (ruminations).

- Hearing voices that are not there (hallucinations).

- Have false beliefs about everyday situations that are not true (delusions).

- Having thoughts of harming or hurting themselves or others.

- Experiencing irrational fear and panic.

- Experience other physical symptoms such as sweating, heart palpitations, breathlessness and pain.

(Adapted from Chaplin *et al*, 2016)

Sometimes, mental illnesses can develop very quickly. If a person appears to have lost touch with reality and is acting strangely or has active thoughts about harming themselves or others, then immediate mental health care should be sought. Accident and Emergency departments have mental health liaison teams who can assess and treat mental health difficulties 24 hours a day, seven days a week.

Assessment challenges

Assessing mental health difficulties in people with learning disabilities can be challenging. This is because the standard assessment process relies on the person being able to give a verbal account of their experiences, thoughts, feelings and timescales, as well as any potential distress. The intellectual and cognitive abilities to be able to do this are complex and involve memory, recall, thought processing, problem solving, understanding of time and being able to understand and respond to questions. For many people with a learning disability, some adjustments to standard interview techniques will help to overcome these difficulties. For example:

- a good use of open and closed questions

- 'anchoring' time to particular events, for example, 'Did you feel like this at Christmas?' rather than, 'How long have you felt like this?'

- asking the same question in different ways and at different times in the interview

- augmenting verbal communication with gestures, facial expressions or using objects, photos or symbols.

However, for those with more significant difficulties, health staff should also rely on family and carers to provide information about changes in appearance, behaviours and sleeping and eating habits, for example. You may be asked to keep a diary or monitoring charts or be asked to support an individual to monitor their own mood using visual scales.

Here is an example of a mood and coping diary:

(Chaplin, 2014)

A visual mood scale, happy or sad:

The information that these charts can provide form a significant part of the assessment process and should be completed accurately and consistently to provide the best evidence.

NICE guidance on the assessment of mental health difficulties in people with a learning disability also states that health staff should be aware:

- *'that an underlying physical health condition may be causing the problem*

- *that a physical health condition, sensory or cognitive impairment may mask an underlying mental health problem*

- *that mental health problems can present differently in people with more severe learning disabilities'*

(NICE, 2016)

The assessment process should therefore be holistic and take account of current physical health and avoid 'diagnostic overshadowing', where difficulties are attributed to the person's learning disability rather than an underlying mental and/or physical illness. Common physical health conditions that can manifest as mental health difficulties are urinary tract infections, an under- or overactive thyroid as well as experiencing pain. Annual health checks and proactive responses to changes in an individual's presentation are key to detecting and treating health conditions in a timely way, and people with a learning disability, carers and family members should proactively seek these out[4].

For some people with more severe disabilities, some signs and symptoms of mental difficulties can present differently. For example:

- skin picking

- hair pulling

- face slapping

- psychogenic vomiting (where the person vomits without any physical cause and it is not self-induced).

These behaviours should be carefully assessed taking account of biological factors such as sleeping and eating habits, appearance and demeanour, and significant life events that may have occurred. A functional analysis and psychiatric assessment could also be undertaken to establish the origin of the behaviours.

It is vital that carers/family members should make sure that they and the person they are supporting are prepared for the appointment. They should ensure that health staff are aware of the learning disability and help them to make reasonable adjustments. They should bring communication aids or items that will help with interaction and communication between the person with a learning disability and the health professional. They may wish to use more

---

4   For more information, see Mencap's *Don't miss out!* available at: https://www.mencap.org.uk/advice-and-support/health/dont-miss-out (accessed December 2017).

formal items such as hospital passports or informal everyday objects of interest to the person with a learning disability that could aid interactions and reduce any worries/anxiety. Support workers and family carers should also be aware that after the assessment or consultation, the person that they are supporting might need extra support because they have had to speak about distressing and upsetting symptoms or events with health staff. Plan extra time to be with the person afterwards to provide support and assurance. It may be helpful to take note of things that have worked well and things that have not worked quite so well, which can then be used to plan for and support someone through future appointments.

Specific conditions

There are many types of mental illness and disorder. The table below looks at four common mental health conditions – generalised anxiety disorder, bipolar affective disorder, depression and schizophrenia – and how they may present differently in people with learning disability. The estimated rates of mental illness among people with learning disabilities for these conditions are:

■ Generalised anxiety disorder: 6%

■ Bipolar affective disorder: 1.5%

■ Depression: 4%

■ Schizophrenia 3%

Mental health problem	Common symptoms	Treatment
Generalised anxiety disorder	The person may be unable to concentrate e.g. follow a conversation or do basic tasks they would normally do with ease. The person may develop irrational fears of everyday situations or doing things that posed no problem before (panic). The person may avoid social occasions because being	The treatments commonly used for anxiety are talking therapies, self-help and self-management, which includes: • counselling • CBT • guided self-help • self-help resources Probably the most commonly prescribed treatment for anxiety is talking therapies based on

Mental health problem	Common symptoms	Treatment
Generalised anxiety disorder (cont.)	with people makes them feel anxious (social anxiety). The person may get physical signs and symptoms such as sweating, pulse racing, stomach upset. The person will become distressed, for example they may be convinced that they are having a heart attack.	cognitive behavioural therapy (CBT). This may include self-help resources either as part of treatment or sometimes as a resource that the person can use independently or with support to manage their condition. Other treatments include relaxation therapy and breathing exercises to help the person to remain calm and relax. For people with learning disabilities this can also involve learning about their symptoms as part of a self-management programme. For those with phobias, treatment will focus on desensitising the person to the object they hold an irrational fear of. In episodes of severe and acute anxiety, sometimes medications will be prescribed for a short period.
Bi-polar affective disorder	The person may have mood swings from being depressed (see above) to being excitable and overactive (hypomania). Some people with bipolar may have mainly depressive episodes. When hypomanic, the person will have reduced sleep or not sleep at all. The person may become disinhibited or promiscuous, or their behaviour may become, extreme, reckless or chaotic.	A number of different treatments are used to treat bi-polar disorder. Often mood stabilising medication is used to prevent symptoms of mania, hypomania and depression. When symptoms are acute, anti-depressants can be used to treat the depression and anti-psychotic medication to treat mania or hypomania. Psychological treatments are often used to target depression and often to make sense of

Mental health problem	Common symptoms	Treatment
Bi-polar affective disorder (cont.)	For example they may take drugs or spend money they do not have. The person may feel or act in a grandiose manner and have feelings of self-importance, or take on jobs and tasks they are not capable of or are unable to complete.	behaviour when unwell and to stay mentally well. For some people, hospital treatment may be necessary if there's a danger the person might hurt themselves and/or others.
Depression	When depressed, a person may: ■ have reduced appetite ■ have difficulty sleeping ■ be unable to concentrate on normal tasks ■ be lethargic and lack energy or motivation ■ stop doing things they would normally enjoy.	Treatment for depression depends upon how severe it is e.g. mild depression might improve by itself or through self-management such as exercise or positive thinking. For mild to moderate depression treatment is more likely to be a talking therapy, such as counselling or cognitive behavioural therapy (CBT). For moderate to severe depression, meanwhile, in addition to these treatments, antidepressants might be prescribed, known as combination therapy. For severe depression, you may be referred to specialist mental health services and, as well as the treatments mentioned earlier, you might be prescribed electroconvulsive therapy where there is risk to the person.

Mental health problem	Common symptoms	Treatment
Schizophrenia	Presentation of schizophrenia is split into negative and positive symptoms. Negative symptoms are likely to appear as chronic symptoms, including: ■ apathy ■ social withdrawal ■ lack of interest in surroundings. Positive symptoms often occur in acute phases where the person may have delusional beliefs, which are false beliefs that are not grounded in experience and that other people do not share and that are unshakeable. They may have hallucinations such as hearing voices that are not there. They may be paranoid or have feelings of being persecuted. The person may have thought disorder – for example, someone is controlling their thoughts or putting in or taking thoughts out of their head.	Antipsychotic medication is usually recommended for the treatment of schizophrenia. Antipsychotics can reduce feelings of anxiety or aggression and other symptoms, such as hallucinations or delusions. Antipsychotics can be taken orally, given as a depot injection, which releases medication over time so the person would have an injection every two to four weeks. Side effects will differ depending on what type of anti-psychotic is used – older typical antipsychotics are characterised by Parkinson type side-effects including shaking, muscle spasms and abnormalities of gait whereas with atypical antipsychotics the side effects will include weight gain. All may cause: ■ drowsiness ■ blurred vision ■ constipation ■ loss of libido ■ dry mouth. Medications should be regularly reviewed. Psychological treatments are also used to lessen the impact of symptoms such as hallucinations or delusions.

Mental health problem	Common symptoms	Treatment
Schizophrenia (cont.)		Psychological treatments are also used to lessen the impact of symptoms such as hallucinations or delusions. They can also improve other negative symptoms, such as lack of motivation and apathy.

Recovery

Care and treatment in the above examples should be delivered within the recovery framework. Recovery is a person-centred concept used in mental health services to describe the processes that someone goes through to either overcome or live with their mental health difficulties in a positive way. That is to say, a process of recovering one's ability to live a fulfilling life, cope with everyday stressors and have hope for and control over one's life. After a period of mental ill-health, it is important that a person with a learning disability is also supported with their path to recovery. Local mental health services can provide support to develop meaningful plans in collaboration with people with a learning disability and their family or carers. Although there is little written about recovery specifically for people with a learning disability, the principles are similar to person-centred planning, so in terms of mental health we need to take into account the signs of poor mental health and triggers to assist early recognition of mental illness and health problems to allow access to early intervention. For successful recovery, it is important that the person with mental health problems takes the lead with support as far as possible in managing their condition.

Key learning points

■ Mental health and well-being affects us all.

■ It is important to promote and maintain our mental health.

■ People with a learning disability may need support to engage in activities that will promote their mental well-being including using the 'Five Ways' to mental well-being approach.

- Mental health and well-being is an important element of care and support as people with a learning disability are more likely to experience mental illness than the wider population.

- Mental health assessments can be a challenge to undertake in some people with a learning disability.

- People with a learning disability are at increased risk of hospital admission and overuse of psychotropic medication if they experience mental health difficulties.

- Support staff and family carers need to be prepared for appointments and ask for reasonable adjustments to be made.

References

Chaplin E (2014) *Self-Assessment and Intervention: The SAINT*. Brighton and Hove: Pavilion Publishing and Media.

Chaplin E, Marshall-Tate K & Hardy S (2016) *An Introduction to Supporting the Mental Health of People with Intellectual Disabilities. A guide for professionals, support staff and families*. Hove: Pavilion Publishing and Media.

HM Government (2008) *Five Ways to Mental Wellbeing* [online]. Available at: https://www.gov.uk/government/publications/five-ways-to-mental-wellbeing (accessed February 2018).

HM Government (2017) *Prime Minister unveils plans to transform mental health support* [online]. Available at: https://www.gov.uk/government/news/prime-minister-unveils-plans-to-transform-mental-health-support (accessed February 2018).

The Royal College of Psychiatrists (2016) *Psychotropic drug prescribing for people with intellectual disability, mental health problems and / or behaviours that challenge: practice guidelines*. Faculty Report FR/ID/09 London: Faculty of Psychiatry of Intellectual Disability, The Royal College of Psychiatrists.

NICE (2016) [NG 54] *Mental Health Problems in People with Learning Disabilities: Prevention, assessment and management* [online]. Available at: https://www.nice.org.uk/guidance/ng54 (accessed February 2018).

Useful websites and resources

Mental Health Nursing of adults with learning disability https://www2.rcn.org.uk/__data/assets/pdf_file/0006/78765/003184.pdf

Foundation for people with learning disabilities
https://www.mentalhealth.org.uk/learning-disabilities/about-us

Mencap
https://www.mencap.org.uk

Royal College of Psychiatrists
http://www.rcpsych.ac.uk/healthadvice/problemsdisorders/learningdisabilities.aspx

Section 3: Topical issues

Chapter 9:

Dementia in people with learning disability

by Marian Jennings

Aims

This chapter aims to:

- understand dementia and its effect on individuals
- analyse the importance of being correctly diagnosed
- consider the impact of dementia on people with learning disabilities and their families and friends
- provide hints and tips on living with dementia.

Summary

- Dementia is an umbrella term for a range of conditions. The early stages of dementia may be difficult to detect.
- Changes in mental and/or physical health need to be investigated.
- People living with dementia need access to appropriate support and services.

Introduction

This chapter considers a range of different issues that affect people who are living with dementia. It will look at definitions of dementia and the issues that face people with learning disabilities, their families and friends when dementia is suspected or has been diagnosed. The chapter will also provide people living with dementia with key hints and tips and it will look at the stories of two people who are living with dementia. The stories will highlight both good and poor practice.

What is dementia?

The word 'dementia' is an umbrella term relating to a range of different disorders including Alzheimer's disease, Lewy body dementia (LDB), vascular dementia and frontal temporal lobe dementia.

According to the Alzheimer's Society, 'the word dementia describes a set of symptoms which may include memory loss and difficulties with thinking, problem solving or language'. Additional issues may include, among others, changes in mood and behaviour, sensory problems, mobility, spatial awareness, hallucinations, confusion over dates/time and mobility issues. Dementia is a progressive condition where treatment is often aimed at delaying the onset of symptoms and slow deterioration of functioning using a range of treatments.

During the initial stages, changes in behaviour and reasoning can be very subtle. The person who has dementia and their family and friends may not recognise that there is any cause for concern.

The Alzheimer's Society estimate that by 2025 there will be a million people living with dementia in the UK and, of those living in England, Wales and Northern Ireland, only 44% will receive a diagnosis.

So why is this important to people with learning disabilities, their family and friends?

Being aware that some people with learning disabilities will develop dementia during the course of their lifetime is important because changes in physical or mental health conditions are frequently overlooked in people who have learning disabilities. Changes are often blamed on the learning disability as opposed to considering other possible reasons. For example, if someone is becoming increasingly forgetful or failing to find the right words, it might be blamed on the learning disability rather than considering other causes such as depression or early onset dementia. It is important to think about the person as an individual and to consider why changes might be occurring.

Failure to detect the onset of dementia in someone who has a learning disability can have a major impact on their life. Poveda (2016) says that the early detection of dementia in people with learning disabilities is vital because an accurate diagnosis can prevent the situation turning into a crisis. An accurate diagnosis will hopefully ensure that people with learning disabilities, their families and friends are provided with the correct support, training, treatment advice and support. This in turn will help enhance an individual's quality of life, enable them to receive effective care, and help people living with dementia to lead an active life.

An accurate diagnosis is also important because experiencing changes in behaviour and physical well-being can be extremely frightening for both the individual and their family and friends. Having a correct diagnosis can help people to make sense of their situation and help them get the correct support and treatment.

The Alzheimer's Society mentions that it is important to assess and identify issues relating to people with learning disabilities because they may have a number of other health conditions that have not been correctly assessed or are poorly managed. People might therefore be living with a range of health conditions and may not be receiving the appropriate treatment or support. People with learning disabilities are also more likely to be wrongly diagnosed or have a late diagnosis of dementia. This delay may mean that the disease has progressed significantly by the time of diagnosis and an individual may have a significant delay in receiving treatment. A missed or delayed diagnosis may cause significant distress to someone with a learning disability because changes may be occurring that they find frightening and do not understand. People with learning disabilities may also have significant difficulty in communicating their fears and frustrations.

People will also need specialist support, for example support from the Community Learning Disability Nursing Team, to understand what is happening to them and to enable them to be involved in decisions about their care.

For some types of dementia, for example Alzheimer's disease, access to an early diagnosis and treatment can help to halt the progression of the dementia. This is a new area of research and at moment it is not known whether these medications are effective in the treatment of dementia in people who have Down's syndrome. More research is needed in this area.

Symptoms of dementia

There is very little research on how people with learning disabilities are affected by dementia. What research there is indicates that dementia symptoms appear to show themselves in the same way regardless of whether or not someone has a learning disability.

The exception is for people who have Down's syndrome – people with Down's syndrome are more likely to develop dementia than the rest of society and they are also more likely to develop dementia at an earlier age. The Alzheimer's society recommends that people with Down's syndrome should be screened for dementia by the time they are 30.

Dementia is characterised by a set of symptoms and is more than just 'being forgetful', but will normally present as a range of neurological conditions that can affect, among other things:

- memory (both long term and short term memory)
- sequencing
- finding words
- sensory perception
- changes in behaviour
- changes in personality
- mood swings
- loss of everyday skills.

Without help and support it can be frightening and isolating for both the person living with dementia and their family and friends.

As dementia progresses, there is also a deterioration in physical ability and functioning, including self-care, to the extent the person will be become more dependent on others for their self-care and to keep them safe from harm.

The importance of an early diagnosis

People with learning disabilities are frequently misdiagnosed because it is assumed that changes in behaviour and understanding are due to their learning disability. For all of us, regardless of whether we have a learning disability, it is important to know how we function on a day-to-day basis. For example, if we have always had a problem remembering names, we shouldn't worry that we have dementia as this is our normal pattern. If you notice that behaviour patterns are changing, or difficulties finding words are increasing, it is important to seek help. Changes associated with dementia are frightening and confusing. An early diagnosis is essential in helping people to get the correct advice and support. This is particularly important for people with learning disabilities as additional support and advice and training for carers, family and friends may be needed at an earlier stage. People with a learning disability may also need additional time to understand the diagnosis. It is vital to provide communication support to someone with a learning disability, and additional prompts and aids to maintain their independence rights and choices.

It is important to recognise that early diagnosis and support will enable the person to maintain a high quality of life and to continue with their interests and activities. Appropriate effective support is vital. Accessible information that provides a clear explanation of the diagnosis is also essential, to help someone to understand the condition, make informed choices and plan for the future.

Both written and spoken communication must be clear and accessible. People living with a learning disability may need pictorial or written prompts to help with memory and sequencing. For example, a picture of a coffee jar or an actual coffee label stuck on a kitchen cupboard, or a pictorial breakdown of how to make a cup of tea. Visual resources such as photos or DVD clips can help people with dementia to engage in activities, make sense of the world and to remember both past and present events.

Accessible communication will also help an individual to engage and make decisions about their treatment, and to plan for their future.

The social impact of dementia

Having dementia can be extremely isolating and people will need to be proactively supported to remain in contact with family and friends and to engage in activities.

Family, friends and support staff may need training and information about dementia so that they have a greater understanding and awareness. Being a carer can be stressful, and if you are supporting someone who has both a learning disability and is living with dementia, it is important that you receive help and support, such as a carer's assessment, respite provision or access to a carers group.

How can I support someone with dementia to maintain their quality of life?

As mentioned, it is important to help people to stay active and to prevent them from becoming isolated. Maintaining a person's social networks will help promote mental and physical well-being and encouraging a normal routine will also help to preserve the person's skills and interests. As a person becomes forgetful or finds executing normal daily tasks more difficult, there are practical things that can help such as breaking down tasks into stages. Also, be prepared to go at a slower pace and give more emphasis to supporting the person to undertake basic checks, such as eyesight and hearing, as deterioration in these senses can have a profound effect not only on ability but also on quality of life.

Key aids and interventions that may help the person with dementia include the following:

- Reality orientation.
- Reminiscence.
- Physical aids and adaptations etc.
- Physical activity.
- Maintaining social contacts.
- Providing clear accessible communication.
- Remembering that continuity is key.

Case study: Lucinda

Lucinda is a 67-year-old woman who lives independently in a house that she has inherited from her parents. Lucinda has a mild form of cerebral palsy and a moderate learning disability. She has lived in her house for the last ten years with the support of a close network that includes her brother and sister, Lucinda's personal assistants and a few of her neighbours. Lucinda has epilepsy and was diagnosed with type 2 diabetes three years ago.

For over 20 years Lucinda has been a regular volunteer at her local hospital. Lucinda travels independently to her volunteering work and really enjoys volunteering at the hospital cafe.

Recently there have been slight changes in Lucinda's behaviour. She is becoming increasingly withdrawn and sometimes seems a little confused, or, as her brother says, 'a little absent'. Lucinda has on occasion failed to turn up for her volunteering job. She is normally very proud of her appearance, however over the last few weeks her appearance has become quite dishevelled.

Lucinda has rung both her brother and sister in a distressed state claiming that someone has been in her house. Upon investigation, the family have noticed that items appeared to be either missing or misplaced, but no evidence of an intruder has been found. Lucinda has recently alleged that one of her personal assistants is stealing money out of her handbag. The PA has denied this claim and seems very upset by the allegation.

Lucinda's family, friends and PA were becoming increasingly worried by Lucinda's behaviour as it seemed out of character and appeared to be more than just being a little forgetful. Lucinda gave her consent for the local Community Learning Disability Team to get involved. She was provided with a complete physical health check-up.

When no underlying physical healthcare problem was revealed, Lucinda was referred for a dementia screening assessment. Before the assessment, its implications were discussed with her. Once again Lucinda's permission was sought before the assessment taking place. The screening revealed that Lucinda was in the early stages of Alzheimer's disease. In order to enable Lucinda to stay in her own home additional support has been provided for her. Lucinda has also been prescribed medication to slow the progression of the disease. The additional support has enabled her to maintain a full social life and to continue with her volunteering activities.

Case study: negative example

Kathryn is a 45-year-old woman with a moderate learning disability. She lives independently in her own flat, is self-caring and needs minimal support. She employs her own personal assistant who visits twice a week, for two hours per session, to support her with her finances, budgeting and paperwork. Kathryn works part time in her local library and is a reliable and enthusiastic worker. She has a long term partner who lives separately and she also has a close circle of friends and family.

Over the last few months, Kathryn's behaviour appears to have changed. She has become more withdrawn and is reluctant to see her parents, her partner or her circle of friends. Normally Kathryn takes great pride in her appearance, however both her personal assistant, her friends and family have noticed that her appearance has deteriorated. She appears listless and is increasingly taking more sick days from work. She also seems to have increasing difficulty remembering sequences, for example how to make a sandwich. On a couple of recent occasions Kathryn has been found by her neighbours wandering around her block of flats in a confused and dishevelled state.

Concerned by the changes in her behaviour, Katheryn's mother persuaded her to visit her GP. At the appointment Kathryn admitted that she was a 'little scared by life at the moment'. The GP dismissed Kathryn's concerns by saying that it was all to do with having 'a learning disability' and that 'everyone one can be a little forgetful at times'. Kathryn left the GP surgery without a follow up appointment.

The impact of dementia is an increasing concern for all of us. If you are person who has a learning disability, changes in behaviour or ability may be overlooked and put down to your learning disability. It is important to recognise and investigate changes in both physical and mental health. An early diagnosis of dementia will enable someone to access the correct support and treatment and to live life to the full.

Key learning points

- Dementia is not a normal part of the aging process. Any changes in behaviour or reasoning should be investigated.

- People with Down's syndrome should be screened for dementia at an earlier age.

- People with dementia are part of an ageing population.

- Dementia affects individuals in a variety of ways. It is not just about memory loss.

- It is important to get an accurate diagnosis and the appropriate support.

- Accessible information and clear communication are vital aids to understanding and empowerment.

- Carers also need support.

- Paid and personal carers need to be provided with dementia awareness training.

Useful websites

The Alzheimers Society – www.alzheimers.org.uk

The British Institute of Learning Disabilities – www.bild.org.uk

The Downs Syndrome Association – www.downs-syndrome.org.uk

Reference

Poveda B (2016) Assessments for dementia in people with learning disabilities. *Learning Disability Practice* **19** (1) pp31–40.

Chapter 10:

Autism

By Jo Delree

Aims

- To understand autism and how it presents in people with learning disabilities.

- To understand behaviours common to autism.

- To have a knowledge of strategies and interventions that can be used to support people with autism.

Summary

Autism is characterised by a 'triad of impairments'. Being a spectrum disorder, the degree to which the elements of this triad affect people with autism is highly variable. This chapter will examine how autism affects individuals, and what strategies we can use to support them and improve their quality of life in terms of making sense of everyday situations and the broader inclusion agenda.

Introduction

What is autism?

Autism is a neuro-developmental disorder that the evidence suggests is caused by a complicated interactions of certain genes and the environment, either before, during or shortly after birth. These genes mean that the brains of people with autism grow and develop differently, which affects how that person understands and responds to the world around them (Chen *et al*, 2015; Geschwind, 2011). This in turn causes people to behave in certain characteristic ways, and we categorise these behaviours as being 'autistic'.

Autism is a 'spectrum' disorder, which means that people with the condition are affected differently – some more mildly and others more severely, each person experiencing a range of different challenges depending on the individual. They may also have other conditions such as dyspraxia, dyslexia or attention deficit hyperactivity disorder (ADHD).

The behaviours that characterise autism fall under the following categories:

- Persistent difficulties with social communication and social interaction.

- Restricted and repetitive patterns of behaviour activities or interests.

- People with autism can also be said to be affected by a 'triad of impairments', which are:

  - social communication (e.g. problems using and understanding verbal and non-verbal language, such as gestures, facial expressions and tone of voice).

  - social interaction (e.g. problems in recognising and understanding other people's feelings and managing their own).

  - social imagination (e.g. problems in understanding and predicting other people's intentions and behaviour and imagining situations outside their own routine).

(DoH, 2010; DoH, 2014)

This is based on the work of Wing and Gould (1979), who first identified the behavioural characteristics of autism. In addition, people with autism can experience sensory over- and under-sensitivities and disturbances, which can have a profound impact on their lives. This means that people with autism can find the day-to-day interactions and tasks that most of us take for granted very difficult.

How many people have autism?

Autism is becoming more widely recognised and the impact that having an autistic spectrum condition can have on the individual and the people that support them is increasingly understood (Crane *et al*, 2016; Baxter *et al*, 2014).

At the present time, people with autism experience poorer health, shorter lives, and a poorer quality of life than the general population (Croen *et al*, 2015; van Heijst & Geurts, 2015; Hirvikoski *et al*, 2016), so it is important that health and social care services understand this condition and that people with autism can get the right support and good healthcare to redress the balance.

Currently accepted prevalence rates are based on the Adult Psychiatric Morbidity Survey 2014 (Brugha *et al*, 2016) and other population studies (Baron-Cohen *et al*, 2009; Baird *et al*, 2006; Fombonne, 2005). The generally accepted figure is about one per cent of the population. This includes people who have a learning disability and autism, as well as those who have autism but do not have a learning disability.

It is hard to establish exactly how many people with learning disabilities also have autism, but it is generally agreed to be around 30% (Emerson & Baines, 2010), while up to 70% of people who are autistic having learning disabilities. Most of this chapter will discuss people who have both autism and a learning disability, but it is also important to know that there are also people who are affected by autism who do not have a global learning disability. That is, they have an average or even above average IQ. These people may be said to have 'high functioning autism' or Asperger's syndrome.

Supporting people with autism

Each person that has autism is unique and the support that they need will be individual to them. In order to get that support right, it is important to understand what the person is having difficulty with, and what is causing them to have that difficulty. To do this, it is useful to look further into the behaviours that characterise autism.

Social interaction

Social interaction for most of us is innate; we have a natural drive or desire to interact with other people and are naturally 'programmed' to look for and respond to other people's emotions and needs. We do not need to be formally taught that an upturned mouth and eyes means 'happy', for example. This is not the case for people with autism.

Research shows us that people with autism are not born with the ability to read emotions from people's faces easily, although again, this is a spectrum and while some people are not able to gauge others' emotions at all, some are able to read simple emotions, and others can be formally taught to read more complex emotions (Chawarska et al, 2012; Carré et al, 2015; Montgomery et al, 2016). An important thing to remember is that most people with autism find doing this hard work. For neurotypical people (those who don't have autism), this is subconscious and requires little effort. For people with autism, because of their neurological differences, this is a process which requires concentration and effort, and for some can be unpleasant and difficult work. Considering this, it is no wonder that some people with autism choose not to interact with other people, but prefer to stay on their own. This is the behaviour that is sometimes referred to as 'aloof' in the literature, based on Wing and Gould's (1979) seminal work.

As well as the differences between individuals, how much social stimulation a person can tolerate can be different depending on what else is going on too; just as a neurotypical person might be calmer and more patient if they have had a good day, but less so if they are stressed.

So, to support people with autism who show us through their behaviour that they are finding social interaction hard, we can:

■ help them to build communication skills – through taught sessions or using non-verbal techniques like intensive interaction

■ socially communicate on that persons' level – if they don't use words, use their sounds, for example

■ give people space – sometimes people just need to be left alone in a safe space

■ give people lots of time to get used to you being near them and to respond to you

■ use social cognition training – using computers or other methods to increase an individual's understanding of social cues.

Case study: social interaction

John is 32 and has a severe learning disability, and does not use speech to communicate. He has just begun attending a specialist day activity service for adults with autism. He lives at home with his parents who are now becoming frail and have found that they are struggling to keep up with his energy levels at home. John's time has been spent almost exclusively with his parents since he left school at 18.

At the day service, staff report that John does not engage with any of the activities he is offered and seems not to want to engage with staff. When he is approached by a staff member he will flap his hands, make a loud humming noise and walk away. John also walks away from other people using the service if they approach him.

Staff are concerned that John seems unhappy there, as are his parents.

Supports for John: social interaction

Staff began approaching John in a different way. Where they had previously approached him with big friendly smiles and lots of verbal greetings, they began to approach more gently and quietly, without using words. First of all, they would simply move closer, not even making eye contact until John was comfortable with them in his space. Then they began reflecting his sounds back to him, even his breaths. This caught John's attention, and staff began to reflect his movement back to him. At first this would last just a few seconds, but as the weeks went past John began to allow staff to come closer to him more quickly, and began to engage more in the interaction, sometimes smiling or laughing, and changing his movements to see if the staff would follow him... and seeming very amused when they did!

This type of interaction is based on a technique called 'intensive interaction' (Hewitt *et al*, 2011).

Social communication

People with autism also have difficulties with social communication. One of the first things that parents of children with autism notice is delayed speech, or in the case of Asperger's syndrome, speech that develops atypically. Some people with autism (generally those that also have a severe learning disability) never use speech to communicate. Others do use speech but this may be limited, or they may be able to use quite complicated speech in specific contexts, but not be able to understand as much as they can say themselves. This is important to remember since it can lead people to assume that the person with autism is more able to understand social verbal communication than they actually are, and they may not be able to understand us if we use the same level of complexity that they do (Hudry *et al*, 2010; Ronconi *et al*, 2016).

People with autism may also use 'echolalic' speech (Roberts, 2014). In simple echolalia, the person will repeat words that they have heard recently without necessarily attaching meaning to them – they are repeated simply as sounds rather than words, although sometimes they may seem to fit the situation by coincidence. Echolalia can be more complex however, with people repeating whole phrases that they may have heard days previously.

Echolia is in fact a normal part of speech development and can be quite useful. When children are learning to speak, they repeat the sounds they have heard and the response that they receive to the sounds reinforces the meaning. The difference is that people with autism may continue this into adulthood, although again this depends on the individual and their ability (Roberts, 2014). In terms of supporting people with autism, this again means that we have to 'listen' in a very different way, observing behaviour as well as listening to words, as what people are 'saying' might not be what they truly mean, they are just repeating sounds. For more able people who use more complex echolalia, it can also add to the perception that the person has a better grasp of language then they really do, and that they understand more than is the case, although recent thinking suggests that echolalia can be used as a learning mechanism to help the individual to communicate (Sterponi & Shankey, 2014).

People with autism also have difficulties with word meanings, even if they do use words to communicate. In the main, this group can understand simple 'labelling' words when they are introduced, although this information is easily forgotten. This part of language development is called 'fast mapping'.

The next phase is called 'slow mapping' and is more problematic for people with autism. Slow mapping involves gaining more experience of a particular word in different contexts, being able to understand more about its meaning and nuances, and also forming stronger memories of the word.

The final stage is called 'extension', and this is where people with autism have the most difficulty. Extension is the understanding that words can extend to whole categories. A cat, for example, is not just one particular creature but applies to all cats, and the word 'cat' overlaps with other categories such as 'animals' or 'pets' etc.

As with all of the difficulties discussed, this varies between individuals, and some people are able to do this better than others. However, the tendency is for people with autism to struggle with language compared to people without autism (McDuffle et al, 2006; Whyte & Nelson, 2015).

This explains in part why people with autism can have a very literal understanding of language. Neurotypical people often use metaphor in their speech; using phrases and expressions such as 'crying your eyes out' or 'raining cats and dogs', both of which are rather alarming if taken literally. But typically developing children somehow know not to take these expressions literally and work out what they are intended to mean. People with autism, to a greater or lesser extent, struggle to do this, although more able people can learn (Marshal & Kasirer, 2014).

Research suggests that this is actually linked to the difficulties that people with autism have with understanding social information and reading social cues from the facial expressions and body language of those around them (Chawarska et al, 2012; Stagg et al, 2014). Because they are not able to pick up social cues, they are unable to make broader sense of words based on context.

This brings us on to the next difficulty that people with autism experience with social communication: a great deal of what we communicate is not communicated through our words but through non-verbal signs such as body language, facial expression and tone of voice etc. People with autism struggle to interpret these non-verbal signs, which compounds the issues that they experience with understanding words, since the two so often go hand in hand.

Often we think we are being very clear in our communication, but on closer inspection, if you remove the social, non-verbal communication that people with autism either don't understand at all, or find difficult and confusing, we aren't.

One persistent myth about people with autism is that they simply 'don't make eye contact'. This is an oversimplified view. While it is true that there are differences in the way that people with autism use eye contact, evidence suggests that it is in fact socially cued gaze that is different, and that avoiding social eye contact is a strategy adopted by those on the autism spectrum because they find it uncomfortable (Tanaka & Sung, 2016). It is more accurate to say that people with autism make atypical eye contact (Senju & Johnson, 2009). This in part explains why people with autism have social difficulties; avoiding social gaze interferes with the ability to process facial expressions and intentions.

If we combine this with other research, which suggests that people with autism find it more difficult to read and interpret social information such as facial expressions, including eye contact (Tanaka & Sung, 2016; Griffiths *et al*, 2017), and that their brains actually respond to and process this information differently (Falck-Ytter *et al*, 2015; Spencer *et al*, 2011), we can begin to understand how differently people with autism understand the world and how much more difficult it is for them to get the information they need to make sense of it.

Supporting people with social communication

In order to support people with autism who are showing us through their behaviour that they are finding social communication difficult, we can:

- remember that the expressive speech of people with autism is sometimes greater than their receptive speech

- keep your language simple and concise, even for people who use fairly complex language themselves

- give people time to respond to you – people with autism process social communication differently and it can take more time and effort to do so

- learn to be quiet sometimes – sometimes the social stuff gets overwhelming

- use pictures signs and symbols – communicate visually

- use objects of reference.

Case study: social communication

At the day activity centre, John is beginning to allow staff into his space. He is still not engaging with many activities, but he seems to enjoy the intensive interaction-style sessions with staff, and he has begun to walk out into the garden. On one occasion he picked up a hand fork and began weeding. Staff have begun to show him the hand fork when they would like to offer him the opportunity to do some gardening – they are using the fork as an object of reference.

Building on this success, staff have begun to try to find other meaningful objects of reference for John to allow him to make more choices and have begun to use objects more generally in their communication – when offering him food and drink choices for instance. If John is shown the bottle of orange squash and the bottle of blackcurrant he will touch the one he would like.

Social imagination/repetitive patterns of behaviour, activities or interests

The world is an inconsistent and ever-changing place, which can be a challenge of all of us at times. None of us like it when our plans change at the last minute, or when something is not where we expected it to be, the bus doesn't come or a friend is late.

Most of us, however, have ways to deal with these situations. We can do something else instead, look for the object somewhere else, get a different bus, or call our friend to see what is happening. We can do this because we have the ability to make the required cognitive shifts and are able to make new plans in that moment based on receiving and making sense of the information from our environment and using our knowledge. These skills fall into the category of 'executive functions'. Executive functions are the mental processes that allow us to think before acting, control our impulses, to adapt to change and unanticipated challenges and to stay focused (Diamond, 2013).

Evidence suggests that people with autism have executive functioning deficits, which contribute to their need for routine and sameness (Miller *et al*, 2015; Vanegas *et al*, 2015). In very simplified terms, neurotypical people are able to adapt to change because we are able to 'imagine' what we could do next, or what might happen next. In other words, we have effective executive functioning. If something goes wrong, or not quite to plan, we can use these mental processes to come up with a solution, and then we know what is going to be happening again.

People with autism struggle with this, so if something changes they are unable to 'imagine' what might happen next. It is extremely rare for a neurotypical person to have that experience, and generally this only happens during extreme (and traumatic) life events. And the feeling that comes with this uncertainty is anxiety.

Research tells us that there is a link between insistence on routine/the need for sameness and anxiety (Factor *et al*, 2016; Joosten *et al*, 2009). Most of us acknowledge that during more anxious periods of our lives, our need for familiar places, people and routines increases. This is exacerbated in people with autism. Although the precise relationships are unclear, it would seem that insistence on sameness and restrictive and repetitive behaviours serves to reduce anxiety for people with autism, and in fact increased repetitive behaviours can be a sign of general anxiety, especially for those with greater social motivation deficits (Factor *et al*, 2016). This suggests that people with autism use routine and ritual to compensate for the difficulties they have with adapting to change – there is no need to do this is if one is following a set routine. However, this also means that a change in routine can cause great anxiety for someone with an autistic spectrum condition.

In a sense, routine is therefore both a support and a challenge when supporting individuals with autism. It can be a tool to support the individual and compensate for social imagination/executive function deficits, thereby reducing anxiety, however a change to a set routine can be anxiety provoking and very challenging for the individual and the people around them.

People with autism may also develop very specialist interests. These tend to take the form of 'collections', either of objects or facts about a specific area of interest (Caldwell-Harris & Jordan, 2014). Experts suggest that this too could be a way of making sense of the world, and people with autism report that they feel comforted when they are absorbed in their special interests (Overskeid, 2016; Spiker, 2012). However, this can also cause problems for people around them when it is not possible to accommodate their interests, or when something goes wrong.

In order to support people with autism with social imagination/repetitive patterns of behaviour, activities or interests we can:

- provide a consistent structure and pattern to the day/week/month etc.

- understand the anxiety that moving away from a routine can have, and always have a back-up plan prepared

- prepare people well for any change using visual communication and other techniques

Case study: social imagination/repetitive patterns of behaviour or interests

After a while, staff supporting John established a relationship with him and he began to engage more in other activities spontaneously. Staff were able to create an individualised weekly plan for John based around the activities he seemed to enjoy.

To do this they used a sequence of objects of reference each day to communicate to John what would be happening and in what order. The objects of reference were arranged in pouches on a wall chart that was exclusively for John's use. John was encouraged to go to this when he arrived so that he could see what would be happening that day. He would then take out the object from the first pouch (the gardening hand fork) and know what he would be doing first. When that activity came to an end he would know what to expect next because he could see it on his wall chart.

Eventually John and his support staff were able to establish a routine of activities that were enjoyable and meaningful to John, and this in turn led to him being much calmer and easier to engage with. Other people in the day centre also used visual supports and wall charts – some of them used pictures, some of them used symbols and some words, depending on what worked best for them and what they preferred.

Sensory sensitivities

People with autism often have sensory processing issues. These can affect any of the senses, including vestibular sense (which is to do with balance and movement) and proprioception (which is about our sense of where our body is in space) (Bogdashina, 2016). People with autism can experience hypersensitivities (being extremely sensitive to particular stimuli), hyposensitive (being extremely under-sensitive to particular stimuli) or they can experience sensory fluctuations and distortions (Wigham *et al*, 2015; Bogdashina, 2016).

This can have a big impact on behaviour. If somebody is hypersensitive to sound, for example, they will react very strongly to noise in order to try and make it feel better; they may cover their ears and make their own sounds to drown it out or they may do anything they can to escape. If they are hyposensitive to visual stimuli, they will seek out strong light, colour, spin shiny things etc. Some people with autism find light touch aversive and even painful, but seek out the sensation of deep touch.

As previously mentioned, these sensitivities can affect any of the senses, and can vary over time, so a person could be hypersensitive to sound and avoiding it one day, and then seeking out loud sounds at another.

People with autism also struggle with 'making sense' of the sensory information that they receive, piecing it all together to make a cohesive whole. This is linked to a theory known as 'central coherence' (Happé, 1996). In short, most neurotypical people have good central coherence. They are able to pick out the important information from the vast array of separate sensations that our senses detect, and assimilate them to form a 'bigger picture'. For example, if we look at a drawing we can detect all of the component parts of the image (the colours, shapes, patterns etc.) and we can see that those visual stimuli all add up to make a picture (of eyes, a nose, a mouth etc., for instance). We can then add up all of those separate parts and we see a face – a whole thing that we understand.

People with autism are considered to have poor central coherence. They struggle with the 'adding up' of all of the individual stimuli. They may get lost in all of the reflected light, or all the different shapes, and not be able to see that it is a face. This is just one example of poor central coherence, and the level to which this is experienced will vary between individuals, but this can apply to anything an autistic person experiences. You may have heard people saying that people with autism find the world confusing – this, and the issues with social interpretation and communication give us an insight into why.

So, to support somebody with their sensory sensitivities we need to:

- understand that sensory difficulties are very real and can be distressing

- understand that hyper/hyposensitivities can fluctuate and be experienced in any of the senses

- provide physical environments that meet sensory needs – usually with neutral colours, natural lighting and minimal external sounds (sounds that the individual is not in control of)

- provide access to sensory stimuli that meet a person's needs

- be aware that we, as people, are very stimulating, and sometimes we may be too much for a person to tolerate

- ensure that the physical environment is kept uncluttered and neutral, and that individual sensory preferences are considered

- make use of various strategies for providing structure and clear visual communication, such as TEACCH or SPELL (Mesibov *et al*, 2005).

Case study: sensory sensitivities

Although John had begun to engage with various activities, staff noticed that he was reluctant to go into the kitchen with other service users when it was time to prepare lunch or snacks. John's parents reported that he was able to do this at home, so staff where initially confused and were fairly insistent on getting him to go into the kitchen with his colleagues.

John's keyworker began to take him in shortly before everyone else came in, and found that John would go in at first and begin the task but would start to shout and leave, pushing past people to get to the door when other people came in.

John's keyworker noticed that it seemed to be the noise of the other people that affected John, the kitchen had a high ceiling and echoed. Along with all the smells of the food, it seemed to be too much sensory input for him. John began to prepare his food before other people, with one member of staff who was aware of the possible over-stimulation and who made sure to keep their voice low. John was also allowed to leave and come back later if it got too much.

Services for people with autism

The Autism Act (2009) states that people with autism require a wide range of services, and that the provider best-suited to meet an individual's needs should provide them, regardless of where they are based (e.g. mental health, learning disability, older adults services etc.). The same principles of inclusion, rights, choice and independence should apply (DoH, 2001), with services being seated within local communities.

Since the range of abilities and need varies between individuals so greatly, what services look like should also vary, however there is wide agreement that staff need a good working knowledge of autism and how individuals may be affected (Rispoli *et al*, 2011; Weinkauf *et al*, 2011; Dillenberger, 2017) and are offered regular training and support.

However, in reality, there is evidence that services regularly let people with autism down (National Autistic Society, 2017). People with autism are often complex, and people and services can find some of their behaviours challenging to support. This has led to people with autism being placed a long way from their families and friends with services that are supposed to be specialised in 'treatment and assessment', treating any mental illness and assessing that person's long-term support needs. These services have come under scrutiny in recent years because of the poor and even abusive practices that have occurred

(Bubb, 2014). Policy has changed in light of these abuses to try and prevent them from happening in future (Glover *et al*, 2014; Bubb, 2014), but change has not happened as quickly as it was hoped (Parish, 2015) and we must acknowledge that some individuals with autism are still poorly supported.

So we must continue to be advocates of change. We must know what should be happening so that we can identify and report poor practice (see Chapters 13 and 14), and so that we can make small changes that can improve quality of life and experience for the individuals that we support on a daily basis.

Case study: real life – when things goes wrong

Alan was a 28-year-old man with autism and a moderate learning disability. He was an only child and has lived at home with his parents all of his life. He is a large man and has some very complex behaviours, and at times he can be aggressive and had hit both of his parents on several occasions, causing them significant injury.

Alan moved from the family home into a supported living service that supported people with learning disabilities, as a place had become available at just the right time and Alan's parents were desperate for a break. An assessment was carried out by a social worker and Alan was moved out of his family home. His mother and father drove him to the new accommodation, unpacked his suitcases, and left.

Alan spent the first night pacing up and down the hall and would not go into his bedroom. When staff tried to approach him he would shout at them and flap his hands at them to keep them away. Eventually, at about 6am, Alan fell asleep in the lounge. Shortly after that other people began to get up and came into the lounge, waking Alan up. He was confused and distressed and began pacing again, this time pushing people who got too close to him. Alan's level of distress increased as more people came into the lounge until he hit a staff member, breaking his nose, and one of the other people who lived in the house, giving her a black eye.

Alan's parents were called and they came and picked him up.

Similar patterns of events continued over the next few weeks until it was agreed that the placement was unsuitable. Alan's parents were so exhausted by this time that they said that he could not return home. An emergency bed was found for Alan on a treatment and assessment unit, where he was taken and given medication to calm him down.

What went wrong?

Because of Alan's parents' understandable fatigue, Alan's assessment was completed rather hastily by the social worker who perceived the urgency of the situation. This, combined with the service provider's keenness to fill a vacancy, meant that Alan was moved from the only home he had ever known with little warning.

This change led him to feel extremely distressed and confused, which caused his behaviour on the first night in a new environment. Essentially, Alan was in a strange place, with strange people, not knowing what was happening to him or what would be happening to him next. He was frightened, extremely anxious, and exhausted.

He awoke in a strange place, still frightened and exhausted to hustle and bustle and noise. This was overwhelming for him, and he did what he felt he could to make people go away; he pushed and then hit the sources of the noise and distress.

His parents coming to get him, although again understandable, meant that Alan never really understood that his was supposed to be his new home. He was never given the opportunity to adapt to the change, and nothing was put in place to support him and help him to understand and establish any structures or communication supports while he was there. The staff in the service were not knowledgeable about autism in general, nor were they knowledgeable about how Alan in particular was affected by autism, and so they were unable to understand and support his behaviour.

The situation was traumatic for the staff, for the people with learning disabilities living in the house, for Alan's parents, and most of all for Alan himself.

Conclusion

It is estimated that 30% of people with learning disabilities have autism. The degree to which autism affects people is highly variable as it is a 'spectrum' disorder, which means that people are affected differently – some more mildly and some more severely. This means each individual will experience a range of different challenges and as a result support needs can also be complex and variable. Common characteristics of autism include persistent difficulties with social communication and social interaction and restricted and repetitive patterns of behaviour activities or interests. People with autism experience poorer health and shorter lives and poorer quality of life than the general population, so it is important that health and social care services understand this condition.

Key learning points

- Autism affects around 1% of the population and is characterised by a triad of impairments: communication, (social) interaction and (social) imagination.

- Autism is a spectrum disorder that presents and affects individuals differently.

- There are a number of key strategies to support people with autism to promote inclusion.

References

Baird G, Simonoff E, Pickles A, Chandler S, Loucas T, Meldrum D & Charman T (2006) Prevalence of disorders of the autism spectrum in a population cohort of children in South Thames: The Special Needs and Autism Project (SNAP) *Lancet* **368** (9531) 210–215.

Baron-Cohen S, Scott F, Allison C, Williams J, Bolton P, Matthews FE & Brayne C (2009) Prevalence of autism-spectrum conditions: UK school-based population study. *The British Journal of Psychiatry* **194** (6) 500–509.

Baxter A, Brugha T, Erskine H, Scheurer R, Vos T & Scott J (2015). The epidemiology and global burden of autism spectrum disorders. *Psychological medicine* **45** (3) 601–613.

Bogdashina O (2016) *Sensory Perceptual Issues in Autism and Asperger Syndrome: Different sensory experiences-different perceptual worlds*. London: Jessica Kingsley Publishers.

Brugha TS, Spiers N, Bankart J, Cooper SA, McManus S, Scott FJ & Tyrer F (2016) Epidemiology of autism in adults across age groups and ability levels. *The British Journal of Psychiatry*.

Bölte S & Hallmayer J (Eds.) (2011) *Autism Spectrum Conditions: FAQs on autism, Asperger syndrome, and atypical autism answered by international experts*. Hogrefe Publishing.

Brugha T, Cooper SA & McManus S (2012) Estimating the Prevalence of Autism Spectrum Conditions in Adults: Extending the 2007 Adult Psychiatric Morbidity Survey. The NHS Information Centre.

Carré A, Chevallier C, Robel L, Barry C, Maria AS, Pouga L, Philippe A, Pinabel F & Berthoz S (2015) Tracking social motivation systems deficits: the affective neuroscience view of autism. *Journal of Autism Developmental Disorders* **45** (10) 3351–63.

Caldwell-Harris CL & Jordan CJ (2014) Systemizing and special interests: characterizing the continuum from neurotypical to autism spectrum disorder. *Learning and Individual Differences* **29** 98–105.

Chawarska K, Macari S & Shic F (2012) Context modulates attention to social scenes in toddlers with autism. *Journal of Child Psychology and Psychiatry* **53** (8) 903–913.

Chen J, Peñagarikano O, Belgard T, Swarup V & Geschwind DH (2015) The emerging picture of autism spectrum disorder: genetics and pathology. *Annual Review of Pathology: Mechanisms of Disease* **10** pp111–144.

Crane L, Chester J, Goddard L, Henry L & Hill E (2016) Experiences of autism diagnosis: A survey of over 1000 parents in the United Kingdom. *Autism* **20** (2) 153–162.

Croen L, Zerbo O, Qian Y, Massolo M, Rich S, Sidney S & Kripke C (2015) The health status of adults on the autism spectrum. *Autism* **19** (7) 814–823.

Department of Health (2001) *Valuing People: A new strategy for learning disability for the 21st century*. London: HMSO.

Department of Health (2010) *Fulfilling and Rewarding Lives: The strategy for adults with autism in England*. London: HMSO.

Department of Health (2014) *THINK AUTISM Fulfilling and Rewarding Lives, the strategy for adults with autism in England: an update*. London: HMSO.

Dillenburger K (2017) Staff training. In: JL Matson (Ed) *Handbook of Treatments for Autism Spectrum Disorder* (pp95–107). Springer, Cham.

Emerson E & Baines S (2010) The estimated prevalence of autism among adults with learning disabilities in England. *Improving Health and Lives: Learning Disabilities Observatory, Durham*.

Diamond A (2013) Executive functions. *Annual review of psychology* **64** 135–168.

Factor RS, Condy EE, Farley JP & Scarpa A (2016) Brief report: insistence on sameness, anxiety, and social motivation in children with Autism Spectrum Disorder. *Journal of Autism and Developmental Disorders* **46** (7) 2548–2554.

Falck-Ytter T, Carlström C & Johansson M (2015) Eye contact modulates cognitive processing differently in children with autism. *Child Development* **86** 37–47.

Fombonne C (2005) The epidemiology of pervasive developmental disorders. *Paediatric Research* **65** (6) 591–8.

Geschwind D (2011) Genetics of autism spectrum disorders. *Trends in Cognitive Sciences* **15** (9) pp409–416.

Glover G, Brown I & Hatton C (2014) How psychiatric in-patient care for people with learning disabilities is transforming after Winterbourne View. *Tizard Learning Disability Review* **19** (3) 146–149.

Griffiths S, Jarrold C, Penton-Voak I, Woods A, Skinner A & Munafò M (2017) Impaired Recognition of Basic Emotions from Facial Expressions in Young People with Autism Spectrum Disorder: Assessing the importance of expression intensity. *Journal of Autism and Developmental Disorders* 1–11.

Happé FG (1996) Studying weak central coherence at low levels: children with autism do not succumb to visual illusions. A research note. *Journal of Child Psychology and Psychiatry* **37** (7) 873–877.

Hewett D, Barber M, Firth G & Harrison T (2011) *The Intensive Interaction Handbook*. London: Sage.

Hirvikoski T, Mittendorfer-Rutz E, Boman M, Larsson H, Lichtenstein P & Bölte S (2016) Premature mortality in autism spectrum disorder. *The British Journal of Psychiatry* **208** (3) 232–238.

Hudry K, Leadbitter K, Temple K, Slonims V, McConachie H, Aldred C & Charman T (2010) Preschoolers with autism show greater impairment in receptive compared with expressive language abilities. *International journal of language & communication disorders* **45** (6) 681–690.

Joosten AV, Bundy AC & Einfeld SL (2009) Intrinsic and extrinsic motivation for stereotypic and repetitive behavior. *Journal of Autism and Developmental Disorders* **39** (3) 521–531.

Lidstone J, Uljarevic M, Sullivan J, Rodgers J, McConachie H, Freeston M & Leekam S (2014) Relations among restricted and repetitive behaviours, anxiety and sensory features in children with autism spectrum disorders. *Research in Autism Spectrum Disorders* **8** (2) 82–92.

Mashal N & Kasirer A (2014) Verbal and Visual Metaphor Comprehension in Autism. In: *Comprehensive Guide to Autism* (pp651–670). New York: Springer.

McDuffie A, Yoder P & Stone W (2006) Fast-mapping in young children with autism spectrum disorders. *First Language* **26** (4) 421–438.

Mesibov GB, Shea V & Schopler E (2005) *The TEACCH approach to autism spectrum disorders*. Springer Science & Business Media.

Miller HL, Ragozzino ME, Cook EH, Sweeney JA & Mosconi MW (2015) Cognitive set shifting deficits and their relationship to repetitive behaviours in autism spectrum disorder. *Journal of Autism and Developmental Disorders* **45** (3) 805–815.

Montgomery C, Allison C, Lai M, Cassidy S, Langdon P & Baron-Cohen S (2016) Do adults with high functioning autism or Asperger syndrome differ in empathy and emotion recognition? *Journal of Autism and Developmental Disorders* **46** (6) 1931–1940.

Moriuchi J, Klin A & Jones W (2016) Mechanisms of diminished attention to eyes in autism. *American Journal of Psychiatry* **174** (1) 26–35.

National Autistic Society (2017) *New Report into Autism Support and Services in England* [online]. Available at: www.autism.org.uk/get-involved/media-centre/news/2017-07-05-autism-support-report-england.aspx (accessed March 2018).

Overskeid G (2016) Systemizing in autism: the case for an emotional mechanism. *New Ideas in Psychology* **41** 18–22.

Parish C (2015) National Audit Office report criticises lack of transfers: Expert panel explains why promises the government made after Winterbourne View were not met. Colin Parish reports. *Learning Disability Practice* **18** (2) 8–10.

Roberts JM (2014) Echolalia and language development in children with autism. *Communication in Autism* **11** 55.

Ronconi L, Molteni M & Casartelli L (2016) Building blocks of others' understanding: a perspective shift in investigating social-communicative deficit in autism. *Frontiers in human neuroscience* **10**.

Senju A & Johnson MH (2009) Atypical eye contact in autism: models, mechanisms and development. *Neuroscience & Biobehavioural Reviews* **33** (8) 1204–1214.

Spencer MD, Holt RJ, Chura LR, Suckling J, Calder AJ, Bullmore ET & Baron-Cohen S (2011) A novel functional brain imaging endophenotype of autism: the neural response to facial expression of emotion. *Translational psychiatry* **1** (7) e19.

Spiker M, Lin C, Van Dyke M & Wood J (2012) Restricted interests and anxiety in children with autism. Autism 16 (3) 306–320.

Stagg SD, Linnell KJ & Heaton P (2014) Investigating eye movement patterns, language and social ability in children with autism spectrum disorder. *Development and Psychopathology* **26** (2) 529–537.

Sterponi L & Shankey J (2014) Rethinking echolalia: Repetition as interactional resource in the communication of a child with autism. *Journal of Child Language* **41** (2) 275–304.

Tanaka J & Sung A (2016) The "eye avoidance" hypothesis of autism face processing. *Journal of Autism and Developmental Disorders* **46** (5) 1538–1552.

van Heijst BF & Geurts HM (2015) Quality of life in autism across the lifespan: A meta-analysis. *Autism* **19** (2) 158–167.

Vanegas S & Davidson D (2015) Investigating distinct and related contributions of weak central coherence, executive dysfunction, and systemizing theories to the cognitive profiles of children with autism spectrum disorders and typically developing children. *Research in Autism Spectrum Disorders* **11** 77–92.

Weinkauf S, Zeug N, Anderson C & Ala'i-Rosales S (2011) Evaluating the effectiveness of a comprehensive staff training package for behavioral interventions for children with autism. *Research in Autism Spectrum Disorders* **5** (2) 864–871.

Wigham S, Rodgers J, South M, McConachie H & Freeston M (2015) The interplay between sensory processing abnormalities, intolerance of uncertainty, anxiety and restricted and repetitive behaviours in autism spectrum disorder. *Journal of Autism and Developmental Disorders* **45** (4) 943–952.

Wing L & Gould J (1979) Severe impairments of social interaction and associated abnormalities in children: Epidemiology and classification. *Journal of Autism and Developmental Disorders* **9** (1) 11–29.

Whyte EM & Nelson KE (2015) Trajectories of pragmatic and nonliteral language development in children with autism spectrum disorders. *Journal of Communication Disorders* **54** 2–14.

Chapter 11:

Supporting people with profound and multiple disabilities

By Renee Francis

Aims

- To explore what profound and multiple disabilities are and how they can develop.

- To identify the impact of profound and multiple disabilities on communication, health and inclusion.

Summary

People with profound learning and multiple disabilities have delayed intellectual functioning and a range of physical impairments which result in a high level of support needs. However, it is important to consider the individuals' strengths and unique qualities when providing support, utilising appropriate communication strategies so that they can express choices. People with profound learning and multiple disabilities are especially likely to experience a range of physical and mental health problems. It is necessary to get to know the person well and to be familiar with their expressive behaviours so that changes in their health or distress can be identified. Supporting people to achieve good physical and mental health, and encouraging positive communication strategies, can help the person to achieve a greater level of social inclusion.

People with profound learning and multiple disabilities have delayed intellectual functioning and a range of physical impairments which result in a high level of support needs. This chapter outlines some of the complexities experienced by people with profound learning and multiple disabilities, and considers the importance of ensuring these individuals are able to achieve inclusion.

What do we mean by 'profound and multiple disabilities'?

People who have profound learning and multiple disabilities have experienced diffuse brain damage. Consequently, they need virtually total support with activities of daily living and have a profound impairment in interacting with their environment and the people around them (Waninge *et al*, 2013). Bellamy *et al* (2010) worked collaboratively with carers, support staff and other professionals to develop a definition of 'profound and multiple disabilities' from a strengths-based approach. They stated people with profound and multiple learning disability:

■ have extremely delayed intellectual and social functioning

■ may have limited ability to engage verbally, but respond to cues in their environment (e.g. familiar voice, touch gestures)

■ often require those who are familiar with them to interpret their communication intent

■ frequently have an associated medical condition, which may include neurological problems and physical or sensory impairments

■ have the chance to engage and to achieve their optimum potential in a highly structured environment with constant support and an individualised relationship with a carer.

(Bellamy *et al*, 2010)

Although people with profound and multiple disabilities might appear totally dependent, they are each individuals with their own personalities, characteristics, likes and dislikes. Likewise, they will each have their own ways of expressing their opinions, and it is important that those of us in a person's circle of support can find ways to give them control over as many aspects of their lives as possible. Creating supportive environments can encourage people to develop their skills and to find ways to express choices (Vorhaus, 2014).

Communication needs of people with profound and multiple disabilities

Every individual has their own way of expressing how they are feeling through facial expressions, body language, behaviour and noises. When someone with profound and multiple disabilities is not able to express themselves through words, these non-verbal forms of communication become even more important. This can leave those of us supporting the person to have to interpret what the individual behaviour or expression might mean. If we are to enhance that person's autonomy, it is important that we make our interpretations in as open and unbiased a way as possible. Phelvin (2012, p35) suggests the following framework for reflection when interpreting a profoundly disabled individual's non-verbal communication:

1. What exactly is the behaviour in question?

2. How do I initially interpret this behaviour – what meaning do I assign to it?

3. What is my initial interpretation based on? How much experience do I have of interacting with this person? What do I know about this person?

4. Why might I interpret this behaviour in this particular way? Do I have anything to gain professionally or personally by this particular interpretation? What do I want this behaviour to mean?

5. Is this behaviour usually interpreted by others (carers, professionals) in a particular way? What is the justification for this?

6. How else might I interpret this behaviour, given what I know of the service user and as far as possible leaving aside my own personal/organisational agenda?

7. How, having asked myself the above, do I now interpret this non-verbal behaviour?

8. Who could I ask, if I remain unsure?

(For an example of how this framework can be used in practice, see the practice examples on p136.)

More formal tools can also be used to support the communication of people with profound and multiple disabilities[5].

Objects of reference are a means of communication in which meaningful objects are used consistently to represent people, activities, events, etc. Objects of reference are used to help people to remember routines, anticipate events and express choices. Their tactile nature makes objects of reference especially useful for people who have both visual and hearing impairments. Computer technology, such as micro-switches, tablets and apps, is playing an increasingly important role in supporting the communication of people with profound and multiple disabilities.

Any communication technique will take time and practice to become established and it is important to give people time to respond. We all appreciate having thinking time when making decisions, even for relatively simple choices such as

---

5   For examples, see www.bild.org.uk/EasySiteWeb/GatewayLink.aspx?alId=3338

what to eat. Consequently, we need to make sure that we allow the people we support this time as well, and don't make assumptions about the person's level of understanding and just carry on regardless.

Physical and mental health

People with profound and multiple disabilities are more likely to experience certain physical health problems than the rest of the population. Many of these conditions are discussed in other chapters, but they include epilepsy, sensory impairment, dysphagia, gastro-oesophageal reflux disorder and constipation. It is important to note here that some of these conditions can be more complex and harder to treat in people with profound and multiple disabilities. Additionally, some of these individuals will experience a number of these conditions simultaneously and they can interact with each other in a potentially harmful way. People with profound and multiple disabilities can be more prone to infections than other people, and a relatively minor illness can have a serious impact on someone who already has complex health needs.

Epilepsy can be caused by genetic conditions, by physical damage within the brain, by metabolic conditions that cause chemical or structural damage to the brain, or by infection affecting the brain. In many cases, the cause of someone's epilepsy is unknown. In people with profound learning and multiple disabilities, the cause of the individual's epilepsy is likely to be the same as the cause of their learning disability. Epilepsy is more common in people with profound learning disabilities than the rest of the population and people with mild learning disabilities. In people with learning disabilities generally, epilepsy is more complex. It tends to involve more than one type of seizure and is harder to control. Outcomes for people with epilepsy and learning disabilities are generally worse than they are for people with epilepsy in the general population (Alvarez, 2015). No individual and their epilepsy will be like anyone else's, so it is important that each person receives good individualised care. This means that carers need to monitor and record epilepsy carefully and consistently, and that people with epilepsy receive regular reviews from their health professional.

People with profound and multiple disabilities are more likely to experience visual and hearing impairments than the rest of the population. Difficulties in communication can make these impairments harder to detect, so it is very important that people are supported to have eye tests and hearing tests. People do not need to be able to speak or read to be able to have their vision or hearing tested.

Due to the physical impairments associated with their condition, people with profound and multiple disabilities can have trouble in maintaining muscle tone and body shape. Postural management uses equipment and positioning techniques to protect and to help restore someone's body shape (Northfield, 2014). Postural management covers all activities that impact on a child's posture over the 24-hour period, including sitting, standing and sleeping. It is a planned approach that would ideally start in early childhood before body shape has distorted. If a person is routinely in an asymmetrical position, they will eventually become fixed in that position. This can cause pain, skin breakdown and restricted access to activities, and eventually can lead to problems with breathing, eating and drinking, digestion and elimination. Postural management uses bespoke wheelchairs and alternate seating in addition to positioning equipment for sleeping to ensure that the individual sits and lies symmetrically. Passive stretching is also used to maintain and develop muscle tone (NWGPPCOT, 2007). Postural management programmes are planned in conjunction with the physiotherapist, and it is important that programmes are followed.

People with profound and multiple disabilities can experience pain and distress, and they are at risk of this not being recognised. Pain can result from poor positioning, pressure, muscle cramps or contractures, indigestion or constipation, or acute illness. It is important to be able to recognise the signs that someone is distressed, and tools such as DisDAT can be used to record baseline behaviours, behaviours when the individual is distressed and possible sources of distress so that the cause of the distress can be addressed or treated.

People with profound and multiple disabilities are at greater risk of experiencing mental health problems than the rest of the population. There is a higher prevalence of affective disorders such as depression in this group. In people with profound and multiple disabilities, this can be more common in people who live in congregate settings, and in people who have experienced major life events (Cooper *et al*, 2007). It can be difficult to pick up when someone with a profound learning disability is experiencing mental ill-health, especially if they cannot use words to explain how they are feeling. Additionally, people make assumptions that those with profound disabilities are unable to process significant life events and therefore would not be emotionally affected by them. This is not the case. People with profound learning disabilities are aware of changes that happen in their lives, and they need support to be able to make sense of these changes as much as possible. This is especially important for individuals who have autism as well. Relating to people with profound learning disabilities as individuals helps us to be aware of important events in their lives, to respond in a way that is appropriate to the person, and to notice any indications that they might be experiencing distress.

Social exclusion

The difficulties that others can experience in communicating with an individual with profound and multiple disabilities can lead to barriers and potential exclusion. This could include exclusion from wider social activities, educational opportunities or employment. Equally, there can be a false perception that people with profound and multiple disabilities do not understand events occurring in their lives or do not have worries or concerns about adverse events. This can create more barriers. Someone might struggle to communicate with the person, but if they also believe that the person is unable to understand, then there is no motivation for that person to try to communicate. Sadly, this can lead to situations where people are not prepared for – or even informed about – major life events such as illness, bereavements or changes in their services.

It is the responsibility of everyone who is involved in the support of people with profound and multiple disabilities to ensure that they do communicate and listen to the person using every available method. Keep offering as many opportunities as possible.

In many cases, families of people with profound and multiple disabilities will know their family member better than anyone else. They will know all of the subtle signs that make up that individual's communication repertoire. It is therefore important to involve family members in order to respond to the individual in the best way possible.

Below are two case examples to illustrate good and poor practice.

Case study: good and bad practice

Good practice

Sally has severe cerebral palsy. She communicates through gestures and some objects of reference. She uses a wheelchair and specialist seating to help her to maintain her shape. Sally lives with her sister who has become ill and is in hospital. Sally has been staying in a local respite service while her sister recovers. Not all of the staff know Sally and so they are not used to her ways of communicating. Adam, one of the support staff, notices that sometimes Sally shouts and waves her arms. He wonders if this might mean that Sally is upset. He moves Sally to a quieter area and she stops shouting. However, she does not seem happier. Adam thinks of other things that she could be trying to communicate, including being excited, being hungry, wanting to stretch and wanting someone to talk to her.

Adam also speaks to other members of staff who have also noticed this behaviour, especially when there is music on. They have also noticed that Sally becomes more subdued when the music stops. They decide that Sally's behaviour probably means that she is enjoying listening to music, and they offer her more opportunities to listen to music and to see a local band in the pub. The next time they are able to speak to Sally's sister, she is able to confirm that she shouts and waves her arms when she is really enjoying herself, and that Sally likes listening to music very much. How could the outcome have been different for Sally if, when Adam moved her to a quiet area, he was pleased that she stopped shouting?

Poor practice

Olu has epilepsy and has a seizure when he is in school. The school staff follow his epilepsy guidelines and he comes out of his seizure well. During the rest of the afternoon, Olu is whimpering. Staff assume that this is because of his seizure and they don't think anything else of it. Later when they support Olu with his personal care, they notice that his foot has twisted behind the foot plate of his wheelchair and is bruised.

Summary

People with profound and multiple disabilities can experience a great many challenges in their lives, but they form strong, lasting relationships with people who get to know them well. Providing the right support, in collaboration with the person's family and friends, to manage communication and health needs can enable the individual to achieve greater social inclusion.

References

Alvarez N (2015) Epilepsy in persons with intellectual and developmental disabilities. *International Journal of Child Health and Human Development* **8** (4) pp493–515.

Bellamy G, Croot L, Bush A, Berry H & Smith A (2010) A study to define: profound and multiple learning disabilities (PMLD). *Journal of Intellectual Disabilities*. **14** (3) pp221–235.

Cooper S, Smiley E, Finlayson J, Jackson A, Allan L, Williamson A, Mantry D & Morrison J (2007) The prevalence, incidence and factors predictive of mental ill-health in adults with profound intellectual disabilities. *Journal of Applied Research in Intellectual Disabilities*. **20** pp493–501.

Northfield J (2014) *Postural care pathway for people with learning disabilities: The Learning Disabilities Elf* [online]. Available at: http://www.thelearningdisabilitieself.net/2014/10/20/postural-care-pathway-for-people-with-learning-disabilities (accessed December 2017).

The North West Group of Paediatric Physiotherapists and Children's Occupational Therapists (2007) *Good practice guidelines to 24 hour postural management.*

Phelvin A (2012) Getting the message: intuition and reflexivity in professional interpretations of non-verbal behaviours in people with profound learning disabilities. *British Journal of Learning Disabilities*. **41** pp31–37.

Vorhaus J (2014) Philosophy and profound disability: learning from experience. *Disability & Society*. **29** (4) pp611–623.

Waninge A, van der Putten A, Stewart R, Steenbergen B, van Wijck R & van der Schans C (2013) Heart rate and physical activity patterns in persons with profound intellectual and multiple disabilities. *Journal of Strength and Conditioning Research*. **27** (11) pp3150–3158.

Chapter 12:

Supporting people with learning disabilities at the end of life

By Renee Francis

Aims

- To explore issues related to supporting people with learning disabilities who are dying.
- To consider the impact of bereavement and loss on people with learning disabilities.
- To apply theory and evidence to practice scenarios.

Summary

People with learning disabilities are prone to a number of conditions that can limit their life expectancy. The individual and their family and friends need to be at the centre of planning for end of life. Planning, co-ordination and collaboration are needed to provide high-quality, person-centred end of life care. This support needs to continue after the person's death to help family and friends cope with the loss of their loved one.

Introduction

When working with people with learning difficulties, we aim to support them to lead full, socially included lives. When we work with people with learning difficulties who are terminally ill, our aim is to continue to support them to lead full, socially included lives while they are dying. This chapter focuses on what is needed to make this happen.

Terms and definitions

'End of life' can refer to the last days of life or it can refer to a longer process. Emmerich (2010) defines 'end of life' as the period when medical intervention can no longer return the person to their stable baseline, and/or when the adverse effects of treatment can no longer be tolerated well. 'Terminal illness' refers to a disease for which there is no cure, and from which the person will die at some point. Some people with learning disabilities have 'life-limiting conditions', which are conditions or syndromes that are usually degenerative and lead to a shortened life expectancy. When someone reaches end of life, they need to be provided with good palliative care. The World Health Organisation (2002) defines palliative care as 'an approach that improves the quality of life of patients and their families facing the problem associated with life-threatening illness, through the prevention and relief of suffering by means of early identification and impeccable assessment and treatment of pain and other problems, physical, psychosocial and spiritual'.

Health conditions contributing to end of life

People with learning disabilities are susceptible to a range of health conditions that can lead to end of life across the life span. It is still the case that common conditions that have the potential to have a greater impact on people with learning disabilities can often be missed. Many of these conditions are discussed in more depth elsewhere in this book.

People with learning disabilities experience chronic and acute respiratory conditions more than the rest of the population. These conditions can mean that the individual is more likely to aspirate and to find it harder to clear secretions from their lungs. Common and relatively mild conditions such as a cold can then put much more stress on the individual's respiratory system. People with learning disabilities also experience a range of gastro-intestinal disorders, including dysphagia, gastro-oesophageal reflux disorder (GORD) and constipation (Friedman, 2010). All of these conditions can be fatal if not managed appropriately. People with learning disabilities are also living longer, which means that they are more likely to experience diseases associated with older age, such as some cancers. For example, people who have GORD are at greater risk of getting oesophageal cancer. Additionally, people with Down's syndrome are at greater risk of acquiring dementia at a younger age than the general population. Multi-infarct dementia and other types of dementia are also more common in the learning disability population as well (Emmerich, 2010).

What are the challenges for people with learning disabilities receiving good end of life care?

Several barriers exist that prevent people with learning disabilities from achieving good end of life care. Diagnostic overshadowing occurs when changes in someone's behaviour or condition are assumed to be due to their learning disability rather than a separate medical reason. These assumptions, along with a lack of knowledge about common health problems in people with learning disabilities, can then lead to delays in diagnosis and treatment. A lack of understanding from health professionals about the Mental Capacity Act (2005), which provides the legal framework around consent to treatment, can also lead to delays. Poor communication can complicate these issues. Assumptions are sometimes made that a person with a learning disability would not cope with discussions about end of life. There can also be difficulties in understanding information, verbally communicating, or understanding an individual's communication styles and aids (CQC, 2016).

Good communication

Good communication is vital throughout end of life care, but it needs to begin as early as possible. It starts with talking to people about death, and being open about the subject. Events in people's lives or in the media, such as the death of a celebrity, can be a way to start talking about death in a natural way, and to support people with learning disabilities to develop a concept of death as being permanent, irreversible and universal. Using the concrete terms such as 'dead' or 'dying' consistently is more helpful to individuals with learning disabilities than using euphemisms such as 'passed on' or 'gone to heaven'. Although euphemisms are intended to be kind, they can be confusing or even distressing to people with learning disabilities. However although it is the responsibility of others to help be as clear as possible, the use of euphemisms by people with learning disability when used appropriately and understood should not be discouraged.

Assumptions should not be made about what an individual with learning disabilities can understand or cope with. People often know when something is wrong, often through other people's expressions (*why is my sister crying?*), through changes in routine (*why can't I go to my club anymore?*), or by how they themselves are feeling (*why do I keep feeling sick?*). It can cause more anxiety and distress if this is never acknowledged or discussed. The key is to give the right information at the right time and in the right amount. Individuals will already possess some knowledge that can be used as a foundation for providing further information (Tuffrey-Wijne, 2013). Everyone processes information at different rates, especially something as important as serious illness and dying.

It is important to be aware of signals indicating when the person has had enough information, and when they are ready for more. It is important to give people time and space to process what is happening, and to allow them to feel sad (Tuffrey-Wijne, 2010). Having the right people available to provide support will help the individual to discuss what's happening in a way that is right for them.

Similarly, people with learning disabilities and the people who support them will need to have information about the process of dying. If family, friends or paid carers have not had experience of caring for someone who is dying, this can become a source of great anxiety for them (PCPLD Network & NHS England, 2017). Gaining an understanding of what is likely to happen will help in planning for the future.

Advance planning

Early discussions with the person and their carers about their needs are important to ensure that care is provided in an individualised, person-centred way, in accordance with the person's best interests. People should be supported to continue doing activities that they enjoy for as long as they can (Tuffrey-Wijne, 2010), and early planning can encourage creative approaches to enable this to happen. Opportunities need to be available to discuss a person's preferred options for the end of life, and to develop their understanding of what the possibilities are. Any plans that are made need to be reviewed regularly, especially when there is a change in the person's condition.

Consideration can also be given to whether any other professionals need to be involved in providing support, and whether any specialist equipment will be needed. This can be an appropriate stage to involve palliative care services, both in the community and in hospices. Early involvement of palliative care professionals can help to build relationships for later on when their input is needed. The better that palliative care professionals know the individual with learning disabilities, their communication styles and their preferences, the more appropriate the care provided will be. Involving hospice services early will give the person with learning disabilities time to visit and become familiar with the environment. This will help them to make decisions about using hospice care in the future. Hospices also offer respite services, which might be a useful option for some people with learning disabilities and their carers. Someone should be identified to co-ordinate care from these professionals and services to avoid confusion and to ensure that the right service is involved at the right time (PCPLD Network & NHS England, 2017).

People who are approaching the end of life, and the people who support them, will want to consider where the person wants to die. People die in acute hospitals, care homes, their own homes, hospices, prisons and secure hospitals. High-quality care at the end of life is possible in any of these settings, with the right planning and support. Central to high-quality care is ensuring that the person's dignity is upheld throughout, regardless of the setting. This includes making sure that they are supported to maintain contact with family and friends, as they wish (Tuffrey-Wijne, 2010). This might include getting in touch with people whom the person might not have had contact with for several years. It is important to respect and support these wishes. Choices about a place to die also need to be reviewed as people sometimes change their minds about their preferred place to die as their disease progresses, and this also needs to be respected.

Pain

Pain can be an area of great concern for those supporting an individual with learning disabilities at the end of life. Pain can be managed well in people with learning disabilities, but it is crucial that everyone who supports the person is familiar with their individual signs that indicate distress and pain. These might include changes in eye contact, facial expressions, vocalisations, muscle tone, sleep pattern or appetite. If someone is experiencing pain, then this needs to be managed promptly. This can be done through medication or through non-pharmacological interventions such as massage or relaxation techniques. Any reversible cause of pain (for example, an ear infection) should be treated promptly (NICE, 2015), so they should be referred to the relevant health professional as soon as possible.

Care in the last days of life

It can be difficult to recognise when someone is entering their last days of life, and it is important to work collaboratively with the multi-disciplinary team to help determine whether the person is deteriorating. As people approach the end of their life they might become agitated, lose weight or have changes in the depth, rate and sound of their breathing. They might be noticeably more fatigued and less mobile, with corresponding changes in their communication and social interactions. They might also have a loss of appetite as the body becomes less able to break down food. It is important to note that these signs and symptoms can change and improve, which could mean that the person is stabilising or even recovering in some cases (NICE, 2015). Symptoms such as nausea and vomiting, breathlessness and anxiety and delirium can be managed with medication and other interventions, so it is important that these are reported to the palliative care team as soon as possible.

As the end of life approaches, people should still be supported to drink if they wish to and they are able to. Mouth care should be provided frequently. The person's need for fluid should be assessed and reviewed regularly by health professionals. Too much fluid near the end of life can sometimes cause problems such as excess fluid in the lungs. It is especially important to be aware of this if the person receives fluid through a PEG or other similar device, as there is a greater risk of providing too much fluid. Decisions about when to stop fluids need to be made in the person's best interests, in collaboration with family and the multi-disciplinary team (NICE, 2015).

Making sure everyone is supported

Caring for someone who is dying can be very emotional. Family and friends need support with their grief, and they will also need time and space to say goodbye to their loved one.

Consideration also needs to be given to the needs of other people the person lives or works with. They will need careful explanations of what is happening, and will need to be given the choice of being involved or not, in being with and supporting the person as the end of life approaches. Their emotions and wishes also need to be acknowledged and supported at this time.

The emotional needs of paid carers and professionals can also be overlooked. Paid staff may have worked with an individual for several years and developed emotional bonds. They might also have little of their own experience of death and dying. It is important that there is appropriate support for paid staff. This might take the form of staff training, supervision discussions, regular staff meetings, or organisational well-being services (PCPLD Network & NHS England, 2017). A clear message needs to be given that it is not unprofessional to grieve for someone with whom staff have worked closely over a long period of time.

After people die

End of life care does not stop when the person dies. Prompt verification and certification of death can be helpful to families and carers. Funeral arrangements can then be made. Ideally, funerals can be planned as part of the advance care plan. Planning funerals early can ensure that the individual's wishes are incorporated into the event.

The family, friends and other people close to the deceased person will be managing their own feelings of grief, even though this process may have started earlier on in the disease process. Support needs to be given to other people with learning disabilities that knew the person well. Each person's experience of grief will be individual, but grief can have some common features. Bereavement can be thought of consisting of two tasks: loss orientation, which relates to traditional activities of grieving, and restoration orientation, which involves making lifestyle adjustments and seeking distractions from grief (Stroebe & Schut, 1999).

People with learning disabilities can often experience compound losses. For example, the death of a parent may lead to the loss of a home if the person needs to move into a form of residential care. This may also lead to the loss of some social networks. It is therefore important that whenever an individual with learning disabilities experiences a loss, action is taken to minimise further losses as much as possible.

All people with learning disabilities who experience loss should be supported with their grief. People with profound learning and multiple disabilities should be included in this support. Particular attention needs to be paid in order to notice signs suggesting that someone with a profound disability is grieving (Young *et al*, 2014). Creative approaches will be needed to support someone with profound and multiple disabilities to express their grief. Multi-sensory approaches can be useful. Working collaboratively with other professionals such as speech and language therapists can help to identify useful communication strategies to help individuals express their grief.

Good practice

The European Association for Palliative Care (EAPC) set up a taskforce to develop Europe-wide norms for palliative care for people with learning disabilities and to collect examples of what good palliative care practice looks like for people with learning disabilities. The task force collaborated with experts in palliative care or learning disabilities across Europe, and developed norms focusing on the following areas:

- Equity of access.
- Communication needs of people with intellectual disabilities.
- Recognising the need for palliative care.
- Assessment of total needs.
- Symptom management.
- End of life decision making.
- Involving those who matter: families, friends, carers.
- Collaboration.
- Support for families and carers.

■ Preparing for death.

■ Bereavement support.

■ Education and training.

■ Developing and managing services.

In the White Paper that was prepared on behalf of the taskforce, several examples of good practice in palliative care for people with learning disabilities from across Europe were used to illustrate how the norms could be put into practice[6].

Case study: poor practice

Maud has dementia which has now reached end stage. She has received all of her fluid and nutrition through a PEG for several years and she continues to do so. Her skin has begun to break down and she has developed a pressure sore in her sacral area.

Maud is now being cared for in bed and has been receiving visitors. She does not interact with them, but she smiles when she hears their voices. Her visitors have noticed that sometimes she seems to tense all of her muscles as if she is in pain. One night she starts to cry out loudly.

When Maud's carers support her with personal care in the morning, they notice that her breathing makes a gurgling sound. When the district nurse visits to change the dressing on Maud's pressure sore, she notices that this has got bigger and explains that this is not unusual as a person gets closer to dying. She makes no recommendations about pain relief. The care staff ask the district nurse about Maud's breathing. She tells them that Maud is probably no longer able to cope with the fluid she is receiving and so they should stop all of her food and fluids. She then leaves for her next visit. Maud's carers are very distressed by this, and worry that they will be starving Maud to death.

---

6   The White Paper can be accessed online from the EAPC website: http://www.eapcnet.eu/LinkClick. aspx?fileticket=Iym7SMB78cw%3d

Organs function less well as death approaches, and this includes skin breakdown. However, appropriate pain relief should be provided to relieve Maud's pain and distress. If Maud is receiving food and fluids in bed and is not being positioned properly, she might be having reflux and then aspirating, resulting in aspiration pneumonia. The change in Maud's breathing could also be related, as the district nurse suggested, and her body is no longer able to cope with the volume of fluid she is receiving. This needs to be assessed properly so that the correct action can be taken. No one from the palliative care team was been involved in this scenario, and they could have provided useful advice about what Maud and her carers could expect. Palliative care is appropriate for everyone at end of life; it is not only limited to people with cancer.

How could the outcome have been different for Sally if, when Adam moved her to a quiet area, he was pleased that she stopped shouting?

Poor practice

Olu has epilepsy and has a seizure when he is in school. The school staff follow his epilepsy guidelines and he comes out of his seizure well. During the rest of the afternoon, Olu is whimpering. Staff assume that this is because of his seizure and they don't think anything else of it. Later when they support Olu with his personal care, they notice that his foot has twisted behind the foot plate of his wheelchair and is bruised.

Summary

Coming to the end of life can be difficult for anyone, but people with learning disabilities need additional support to help them achieve a good death. Family, friends, paid carers and professionals all have a role in this. Working in partnership with the individual and their loved ones to find out what is important to them at end of life will help to provide good person-centred end of life care.

References

Care Quality Commission (CQC) (2016) *A Different Ending: People with a learning disability* [online]. Available at: http://www.cqc.org.uk/sites/default/files/20160505%20CQC_EOLC_LearningDisabilities_FINAL_2.pdf (accessed December 2017).

Emmerich M (2010) Medical conditions in adults near the end of life. In: S Friedman and D Helm (eds) *End-of-Life Care for Children and Adults with Intellectual and Developmental Disabilities*. Washington: American Association on Intellectual and Developmental Disabilities pp75-91.

Friedman S (2010) Complex medical problems affecting life and life span in children. In: S Friedman & D Helm (eds) *End-of-Life Care for Children and Adults with Intellectual and Developmental Disabilities*. Washington: American Association on Intellectual and Developmental Disabilities pp53–73.

National Institute of Health and Care Excellence (NICE) (2015) *Care of Dying Adults in the Last Days of Life* [online]. Available at: https://www.nice.org.uk/guidance/ng31 Accessed 16/08/2017 (accessed December 2017).

PCPLD Network & NHS England (2017) *Delivering high quality end of life care for people who have a learning disability: Resources and tips for commissioners, service providers and health and social care staff* [online]. Available at: https://www.england.nhs.uk/publication/delivering-high-quality-end-of-life-care-for-people-who-have-a-learning-disability/ (accessed December 2017).

Stroebe M & Schut H (1999) The dual process model of coping with bereavement: rationale and description. *Death Studies* **23** pp197–224.

Tuffrey-Wijne I (2010) *Living with Learning Disabilities, Dying with Cancer: Thirteen personal stories*. London: Jessica Kingsley Publishers.

Tuffrey-Wijne I (2013) *How to Break Bad News to People with Intellectual Disabilities : A guide for carers and professionals*. London: Jessica Kingsley Publishers.

World Health Organization (2002) *WHO definition of palliative care* [online]. Available at: http://www.who.int/cancer/palliative/definition/en/ (accessed December 2017).

Young H, Garrard B, Lambe L & Hogg J (2014) Helping people cope with bereavement. *Learning Disability Practice* **17** (6) pp16–20.

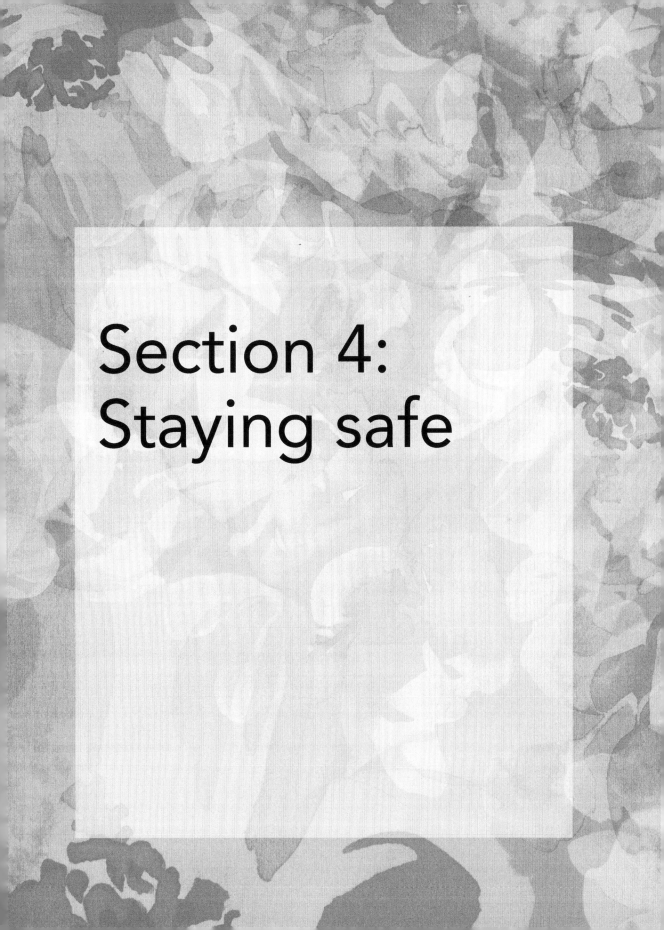

Section 4:
Staying safe

Chapter 13:

Safeguarding adults with learning disabilities: what is abuse?

By Andy Mantell, Gill Concannon and Peter Warburton

Aims

To ensure awareness of the 10 categories of abuse included in the Care Act (2014) and to know what signs to look out for that may indicate abuse is occurring in people with learning disabilities.

To identify potential abusers and the circumstances that increase the risk of abuse for people with learning disabilities.

Summary

This chapter explores safeguarding in relation to people with learning disabilities. In order to be able to prevent abuse of people with learning disabilities from happening, it is critical to be aware of different forms of abuse and to be sensitive to their indicators. This chapter highlights the different categories of abuse and their particular implications for people with learning disabilities. Through the use of case studies, it also illustrates how safeguarding issues are resolved in order to protect individuals. Safeguarding is viewed from a life course perspective, rather than viewing safeguarding children, adults and domestic abuse in isolation. It should be read in conjunction with the following chapter on what to do and how to prevent abuse.

Introduction

This chapter focuses on safeguarding adults with learning disabilities, however it is important to understand safeguarding as an issue across the life-course, rather than viewing safeguarding children, adults and domestic abuse in isolation. The different stages in the life course present different safeguarding challenges for people with learning disabilities, for example when exploring sexuality, during the transition stage from home to independence or when the need for complex care for co-morbidity in older life arises. Many themes are the same in adulthood or childhood, for example the abuse of power. Much can be learnt from other fields of practice such as strengths based approaches in child protection, including *Signs of Safety* (Edwards & Turnell, 1999; Lindon & Webb, 2016). This approach shifts the focus from familial deficits, such as lack of parenting skills, to how their resources can be used to keep a child safe, for example involving the extended family in supporting them. Most importantly, practitioners need to remember to look beyond the person who is their primary concern – for example, where an adult with learning disabilities is at risk of abuse it is essential to also consider if other adults or children could also be deemed at risk.

What is abuse?

Abuse is where a person is caused harm, which may be to their emotional, psychological, sexual, physical or material well-being. The Care Act (2014) divides abuse into ten categories. These are listed below with examples, possible indicators of abuse and the implication of this type of abuse for those with learning disabilities. When considering possible indicators or signs of abuse, be aware that they may range from observable injuries or loss of money or possessions, to emotional and psychological indicators such as changes in mood, behaviour and a person's general demeanour. A person may also experience several types of abuse simultaneously. However, also be mindful that the changes of behaviour mentioned above do not necessarily mean that abuse has occurred. Below are listed types of abuse and examples of the differing ways they are perpetrated, and how we might recognise there is a safeguarding issue.

Physical abuse – is the pain or injury caused by a person's action or inaction. Examples include hitting and misuse of medication. Possible indicators include unexplained injuries or the adult showing fear or distress. People with learning disabilities have been particularly susceptible to misuse of medication and/or excessive use of restraint and overt violence, for example at Winterbourne View Hospital (Flynn, 2012). The abuse of people with learning disabilities can be attributed to work place cultures in which they are not valued and reflects wider social discrimination. A CQC (2016) review into the deaths of people in NHS trusts care found that 'the level of acceptance and sense of inevitability when people with a learning disability or mental illness die early is too common'.

Sexual abuse – direct or indirect sexual activity without the person's consent. Examples include rape and inappropriate touching. Possible indicators include changes in behaviour, sudden incontinence and sexually transmitted diseases.

Withers and Morris (2012) suggest that between 25 and 50% of adults with learning disabilities have been sexually exploited, with almost 1,400 new cases occurring in the UK each year. This high prevalence may be partly due to staff tolerating levels of inappropriate and abusive behaviour between people with learning disabilities that they wouldn't tolerate in the general population (Lyall *et al*, 1995).

Psychological (and emotional) abuse – it is important to distinguish between a person's emotional distress and the psychological impact on their sense of self-worth and identity. Examples include threats of harm or abandonment and intimidation. Possible indicators include anxiety and withdrawal. Systematic abuse often remains unidentified and unrecognised by both the recipient and the alleged cause of risk. The resulting cumulative impact of psychological and emotional abuse and neglect is deep rooted and embedded in poor practice and service culture. For instance, a person with repetitive speech or routines that overtime become wearisome to others may subsequently lead them to being either ignored completely or dismissed. This interaction becomes the norm but is nonetheless an abusive negative stance, which impacts on a persons' feeling of self-worth.

Financial abuse – the improper use of money or assets. Examples include theft or changing a person's will. Possible indicators include unexplained shortages of money or a lack of food in their home. For example, a brother who helped his disabled sister set up internet banking knew her personal identification details and later embezzled money from her account. This situation was only discovered when insufficient funds were available to pay for her holiday. Financial gain is often a factor in 'mate crime', where a person befriends someone with the aim of exploiting them. The person who is being exploited may not view themselves as such and may see the person who causes these concerns as their friend. People with learning disabilities are particularly at risk of being targeted (Landman, 2014), as they may be viewed as easier to manipulate.

Neglect and acts of omission – the deliberate or unintentional failure to provide adequate care. Gross failures in duty of care are ill treatment and wilful neglect and are punishable with up to five years in prison (Criminal Justice and Court Acts (2015)). Examples would be over/under medicating and causing malnutrition. Possible indicators include poor hygiene and inadequate physical environment.

Discriminatory abuse – the exploitation of a person's characteristics to exclude them from opportunities in society. This discrimination can relate to any of the protected characteristics under the Equality Act (2010): age, disability, gender reassignment, marriage and civil partnership, pregnancy and maternity, race, religion and belief, sex and sexual orientation. Examples include unequal treatment and harassment. Possible indicators include lack of respect and exclusion from services. Hate crime can be seen as an extreme form of discriminatory abuse (see Chapter 16).

Organisational abuse – formerly known as institutional abuse, organisational abuse is where an organisation's systems, processes and/or management, fails to safeguard an individual. Organisational abuse can also occur when the routines, systems and norms of an organisation override the needs of those it is there to support, or fail to provide those individuals with an appropriate quality of care. Examples include a lack of dignity and lack of access to care. Indicators include a controlling relationship between staff and people with learning disabilities and a lack of flexibility by staff. Organisational abuse highlights how the quality of services plays a pivotal role in either preventing or contributing to abusive care. However, the statuary guidance to the Care Act (2014) (Department of Health, 2017) is clear that safeguarding procedures should not be used as a substitute for service providers' responsibilities to provide high-quality care and support.

Self-neglect – is the inability to maintain socially and culturally accepted standards of care. At its severest, examples include psychological disorders such as hoarding (accumulating and failing to discard items others deem of limited value) or Diogenes disease (domestic squalor or extreme self-neglect). Possible indicators include a very unclean environment and eccentric and compulsive hoarding. Note that self-neglect would not usually be responded to under section 42 of the Care Act (2014) (see Chapter 14), which tends to relate to abuse by others. Withdrawing on the basis that that is their choice risks the behaviour becoming entrenched and escalating. SCIE (2014) found there is no conclusive evidence about what works best for supporting people who self-neglect, but they recommend relationship-based working – 'sensitivity and gentle persistence', building trust and utilising a multi-agency approach (Braye *et al*, 2011).

Domestic abuse – formerly known as domestic violence, this is 'any incident or pattern of incidents of controlling, coercive, threatening behaviour, violence or abuse between those aged 16 or over who are, or have been, intimate partners or family members regardless of gender or sexuality. The abuse can encompass, but is not limited to psychological, physical, sexual, financial, emotional' (HM Government, 2016). The person who is at risk can be 16 or over (for those under 18, child safeguarding procedures apply). The person who is the cause of the risk may be of any gender and may be an adult or a child. Domestic abuse would only trigger adult safeguarding procedures if the adult at risk has care needs that prevent them from protecting themselves, such as a severe learning disability. In other cases, domestic abuse procedures would be triggered, including Multi-Agency Risk Assessment Conferences (MARAC) to look at how to best support the adult. If the person who is the cause of risk is a sexual or violent offender then Multiple Agency Public Protection Arrangements (MAPPA) to manage the risk they pose would be reviewed. 'Controlling and coercive behaviour in an intimate or family relationship' is now a criminal offence, which can lead to five years in prison (Serious Crime Act (2015)). Note that if a child witnesses domestic abuse they have met the criteria for significant harm (Adoption and Children Act (2002)), requiring the involvement of children's services. Examples of domestic abuse include physical and sexual violence. Possible indicators include isolation and constant criticism.

Modern slavery – an international crime involving a substantial number of source and transit countries. Organised crime groups systematically exploit large numbers of individuals by forcing and coercing them into a life of abuse and degradation (Home Office, 2016). The Modern Slavery Act (2015) introduced a sentence of up to life in prison and encourages the seizing of assets and compensation for the victims. Examples include human trafficking, where people from abroad with and without a learning disability are exploited in the sex industry, forced labour, domestic servitude in the home and forced criminal activity. It can also include adults from this country, in particular those who had previously suffered child sexual exploitation or people who have learning disabilities who may be intimidated or manipulated into modern slavery. Possible indicators include living in squalid, overcrowded conditions and being isolated and reluctant to speak to, or prevented from speaking to others, being escorted to health appointments and frequent attendances at sexual health clinics, not having their own passport or documentation.

While the Care Act lists the above categories of abuse, contained within them are distinct types of abuse, which are important to note.

Deprivation of liberty – (psychological and/or physical abuse) removing a person's freedom is a form of abuse and only allowed under legal authorisation, for example where someone has committed a crime or where they are detained under the Mental Health Act (1983) (as amended by the Mental Health Act (2007)). In other circumstances, where a person lacks mental capacity, Deprivation of Liberty Safeguards (DoLS) must be put in place.

Case study: P

P, who has cerebral palsy and Down's syndrome, lacked the mental capacity to make decisions about his care and residence. He lived in a supported living bungalow with other residents, where he received substantial one-to-one care and supervision. He was also subject to physical interventions to manage behaviours, including tearing up his incontinence pads and putting the pieces in his mouth (Valios, 2014).

Before looking at the next stage, ask whether you think P was experiencing a deprivation of his liberty?

Comment

The Court of Appeal had said that this was not a deprivation of liberty because P's life was as normal as possible for someone with his level of disability and he would require the same level of supervision in any other setting. However, the Supreme Court rejected this unanimously, saying disabled people should not face a tougher standard for being deprived of their liberty than non-disabled people (Valios, 2014).

This landmark judgement produced a new set of criteria for determining if a person is being deprived of their liberty:

■ Do they lack the capacity to consent to their care/treatment arrangements?

■ Are they under continuous supervision and control?

■ Are they not free to leave?

(Cheshire West and Chester Council v P [2014] UKSC 19 [2014] MHLO 16)

DoLS may be in the form of a standard authorisation, which lasts up to 12 months or emergency authorisation, which lasts up to seven days (The Mental Capacity Act (2005), as amended by the Mental Health Act (2007)). However, if a person is in their own home then detention would require authorisation by the Court of Protection.

Hate crime – a hate incident is any incident which the victim, or anyone else, thinks is based on someone's prejudice towards them because of their race, religion, sexual orientation, disability or because they are transgender (Home Office, 2016).

'Honour'-based violence – (domestic abuse) includes physical and/or sexual violence to a person in the belief that this will protect the family or community's reputation. 'Honour' killing is where the person is killed for being perceived to have brought shame upon the family. 'Honour' crimes are strongly linked to forced marriages (see below).

Female Genital Mutilation (FGM) – a form of physical abuse also known as female circumcision and 'cutting'. FGM involves the cutting, injuring or changing of the female genitals. There are four main types of FGM: clitoridectomy (removing the clitoris), excision (removing part or all of the clitoris and the inner labia), infibulation (narrowing the vaginal opening, to create a seal, by cutting and repositioning the labia) and other forms of mutilation, such as piercing, cutting scrapping or burning their genitalia. Usually it is carried out without consent and without anaesthetic by a person without medical training, using a range of implements from glass to scissors and razor blades. FGM is usually carried out on girls between infancy and puberty. It serves no medical purpose, but can cause physical problems such as constant pain and difficulties in giving birth and can lead to mental health issues, such as depression and flash backs. Conducting FGM, or taking a person abroad for FGM is illegal in the UK and carries a sentence of up to 14 years under the Female Genital Mutilation (FGM) Act (2003). The Serious Crimes Act (2015) amended the FGM Act (2003) to introduce FGM Protection Orders, breaches of which carry up to five years in prison. The Act introduced a legal duty on health and social care professionals and teachers to report when told by a girl under 18 that she has had FGM or even if they see physical signs that FGM has been conducted. Curiously, it does not apply if she is over 18 and discloses that FGM happened at a younger age. The legal duty of health care professionals does not apply to women who are 18 or older, but safeguarding adult procedures still apply (see Chapter 14).

Forced marriage – (child/adult sexual abuse, as well as psychological and physical abuse) this should not to be confused with arranged marriage, where the individuals have a choice whether to go ahead with the marriage. Forced marriage is where an individual is coerced into marriage by physical intimidation (threats of physical or sexual violence) psychological coercion (fear of bringing disgrace upon the family) or material deprivation (preventing them accessing money or resources). This may occur to children as well as adults. One reason proffered by victims is to prevent them entering into 'unsuitable relationships' for example, where a person is gay. The Antisocial Behaviour, Crime and Policing Act (2014) made it a crime to force someone to marry.

Case study: SA

SA was an 18-year-old woman with a mild learning disability and a reading age of about seven. Profoundly deaf, she communicated using British Sign Language and lip-reading English. She lived with her family who originated from Pakistan, and her first language was Punjabi. Her parents wanted to take her to Pakistan for an arranged marriage. However, the local authority intervened by applying to the Court of Protection to prevent it happening.

Justice Munby (Re SA (Vulnerable Adult with Capacity: Marriage) [2005] EWHC 2942) Fam) considered that any other vulnerable adult could come under the jurisdiction of the Court of Protection. He considered that although SA generally had the capacity to decide whether to marry or not, in these circumstances she was experiencing situational incapacity. The Court of Protection defined three types of situational incapacity:

■ 'Constraint' – curtailment of freedom of activity.

■ 'Coercion or undue influence' – particularly based on affection, duty, obligation or social, cultural or religious beliefs.

■ 'Other disabling circumstances' – which 'may so reduce a vulnerable adult's understanding and reasoning powers as to prevent him from forming or expressing real and genuine consent, for example, the effects of deception, misinformation, physical disability, illness, weakness (physical, mental or moral), tiredness, shock, fatigue, depression, pain or drugs. No doubt there are others.'

In SA's case all three types of situational capacity were found to apply. This ruling provides protection to people with learning disabilities who may be coerced by others. However, the circumstances in which it could apply are extremely broad.

Information and Communication Technology (ICT) abuse – (may be a form of sexual abuse and or financial abuse) involving social media and webpages, using computers, mobile phones, tablets and webcams to cause harm to an individual. This may be through exposure to *content* such as pornography; enticement to *contact* with others, for example, meeting others and sexual grooming; or guiding their *conduct*, for example by making and posting sexual material.

Mate crime – (a form of discriminatory abuse, often linked to financial abuse) is the exploitation, abuse or theft from a person by those they consider to be their friends. People with learning disabilities are particularly likely to be targeted for this type of abuse. A lack of knowledge about what makes a good relationship appears to be a major reason for people with learning disabilities engaging in dangerous sexual relationships (Dukes & McGuire, 2009; Tullis & Zangrillo, 2013). It has been suggested that many non-disabled people learn as much about sex from friends, family and social networking sites as they do from formal education (Jahoda & Pownall, 2013). This is not the case for people with learning disabilities who tend to have much smaller social networks and appear to gain much of their sex education from what they observe in their own families and mainstream media (Jahoda & Pownall, 2013). A person with a learning disability who is sexually assaulted by a relative or 'friend' is less likely to have friends to compare experiences with.

Stalking – (form of psychological abuse) is not legally defined, but examples include following, watching and spying upon a person. The Protection from Harassment Act (1997) was amended by the Protection of Freedoms Act (2012) to include two new offences of stalking.

Terrorism – Although terrorism would not be dealt with under safeguarding proceedings, the government's Prevent programme (part of the Contest strategy) (Home Department, 2011) is aimed at stopping the grooming of people who may be more susceptible to manipulation and grooming to become radicalised (a process of slowly befriending and crossing boundaries in order to persuade or coerce a person into unwanted behaviours). People with mild learning disabilities would be at risk of such exploitation.

Who abuses?

The following is a list of people who might abuse:

- People who deliberately exploit adults they perceive as 'vulnerable'.
- Spouses or partners.
- Other family members.
- Neighbours.
- Friends.
- Acquaintances.
- Local residents.
- Paid staff or professionals.
- Volunteers and strangers.
- An adult with care and support needs.

When we think of abusers, we may well think of those who set out to deliberately target and abuse people, but anyone might abuse. Consequently, it is better to focus on abusive traits displayed by those who cause risk. This may range from a lack of insight and an inability to learn from mistakes, to unreliability, irresponsibility, self-centeredness and, at its extreme, predatory behaviour and grooming (a process of gradual befriending and blurring of boundaries aimed towards exploitation).

Note that there are two common themes in those who cause risk: a lack of empathy and/or a lack of competence.

These two factors can be related, for example a person may not be aware that they lack competence, or they may be aware but not care due to a lack of empathy for those they care for. In contrast, a person who is a cause of risk may be very competent, with extremely good people skills which they use to gain an individual's trust for their own ends. This is particularly the case in 'mate crime', where they befriend the person to exploit them.

What factors increase or reduce a person's risk of abuse?

Factors that are associated with risk of abuse can be grouped into personal, relationship and environmental factors.

Table 2: Factors that affect the risk of abuse

Personal	Relationship	Environmental
Poor communication or communication difficulties.	Unequal power relationships (that include controlling, coercive or threatening behaviour).	Overcrowding.
History of falls and/or minor injuries.	History of violent relationships within the family or social networks.	Poor or insecure living conditions.
Physical and/or emotional dependence on others.	Increased reliance on others by the person.	Homelessness.
Mental health needs, including dementia.	Reliance on more than one person within the family or social networks.	Poor management.
Lacking capacity to make key decisions.	Multi-generational family structure where conflicts of interest and loyalties may exist.	High staff turnover.
Rejection of help.	Role reversal or significant change in the relationship between the person and their carer.	Insufficient staff.
Aggression.	History of abuse within the family, either being abused or responsible for previous abuse.	Geographical or social isolation.
Self-injurious behaviour.	Isolation of the carer due to the demands of caring, leading to a lack of practical and emotional support.	Other adults with challenging behaviour.

Personal	Relationship	Environmental
History of repeatedly making allegations of abuse.	Lack of understanding about the person's condition, resulting in inappropriate care.	Organisational and wider cultural attitudes that stigmatise and/or do not value particular groups, such as those with learning disabilities.
High level of reliance on others for care or finances.	Difficult or challenging behaviour by the person that the carer finds intolerable or stressful, or which puts the carer at risk.	
Substance misuse.	Financial difficulties.	
Being a carer.	Illness or disability of the carer.	
	Significant and long-term stress of the carer.	
	Inappropriate care responses e.g. poor quality care, support or treatment.	

This list of factors is generic rather than specifically related to people with learning disabilities, however there is a high prevalence of these factors among people with learning disability. Brown's (2009) review of serious case reviews (now safeguarding adults reviews) found that people with learning disabilities and older people with dementia were the two largest groups of adults that were subject to serious case reviews. As Brown (2009) notes, this may be reflective of deficits in wider social values related to these groups.

The relationship between these factors is complex and should be viewed simply as a causal relationship, for example rejection of help may be because they are being abused rather than being a contributing factor to abuse occurring.

Key learning points

This chapter has explored the diverse ways in which people with learning disabilities are abused. It has highlighted possible indicators of abuse and factors that can increase the potential for abuse to occur. The next chapter will look at how abuse can be prevented and what to do when it occurs. However, without raising awareness of abuse, it will continue to go unnoticed, ignored or even tolerated.

References

Braye S, Orr D & Preston-Shoot M (2011) *Self-neglect and Adult Safeguarding: Findings from research* [online]. Available at: http://www.scie.org.uk/publications/reports/report46.pdf (accessed December 2017).

Brown H (2009) The process and function of serious case review. *Journal of Adult Protection* **11** (1) 38–50.

Cheshire West and Chester Council v P [2014] UKSC 19 [2014] MHLO 16. Available at: https://www.supremecourt.uk/decided-cases/docs/UKSC_2012_0068_Judgment.pdf

CQC (2016) *Learning, Candour and Accountability. A Review of the Way NHS Trusts Review and Investigate the Deaths of Patients in England* [online]. Available at: http://www.cqc.org.uk/sites/default/files/20161213-learning-candour-accountability-full-report.pdf (accessed December 2017).

Department of Health (2017) *Care and Support Statutory Guidance*. Available at: https://www.gov.uk/government/publications/care-act-statutory-guidance/care-and-support-statutory-guidance (accessed December 2017).

Dukes E & McGuire B (2009) Enhancing capacity to make sexuality-related decisions in people with an intellectual disability. *Journal of Intellectual Disability Research* **53** (8) 727–734.

Edwards S & Turnell A (1999) *A Solution and Safety Orientated Approach to Child Protection Case Work*. New York: W. W Norton and Company.

Flynn M (2012) *South Gloucestershire Safeguarding Adult Board Winterbourne View Hospital: A serious case review* [online]. Available at: http://www.hampshiresab.org.uk/wp-content/uploads/2012-Serious-Case-Review-regarding-Winterbourne-View-South-Gloucestershire.pdf (accessed December 2017).

HM Government (2016) *Domestic Violence and Abuse* [online]. Available at: https://www.gov.uk/guidance/domestic-violence-and-abuse#domestic-violence-and-abuse-new-definition (accessed December 2017).

Home Office (2016) *Action Against Hate: The UK Government's plan for tackling hate crime* [online]. Available at: https://www.gov.uk/government/uploads/system/uploads/attachment_data/file/543679/Action_Against_Hate_-_UK_Government_s_Plan_to_Tackle_Hate_Crime_2016.pdf (accessed December 2017).

Home Department (2011) *Prevent Strategy* [online]. Available at: https://www.gov.uk/government/uploads/system/uploads/attachment_data/file/97976/prevent-strategy-review.pdf (accessed December 2017).

Jahoda A & Pownall J (2014) Sexual understanding, sources of information and social networks: the reports of young people with intellectual disabilities and their non-disabled peers. *Journal of Intellectual Disability Research* **58** (5) 430–441.

Landman R (2014) "A counterfeit friendship": mate crime and people with learning disabilities. *Journal of Adult Protection* **16** (6) pp355–366.

Lindon J & Webb J (2016) *Safeguarding and Child Protection 5th Edition: Linking theory and practice*. Hachette UK.

Lyall A, Holland A & Collins S (1995) Offending by adults with learning disabilities and the attitudes of staff to offending behaviour: implications for service development. *Journal of Intellectual Disabilities* **39** (6) 501–508.

Re SA (Vulnerable Adult with Capacity: Marriage) [2005] EWHC 2942) Fam. MARRIAGE: Re SA (Vulnerable Adult with Capacity: Marriage) [2005] EWHC 2942 (Fam). Available at: http://www. familylaw.co.uk/news_and_comment/re-sa-vulnerable-adult-with-capacity-marriage-2005-ewhc-2942-fam#.WNPp_IXXLIU (accessed February 2018).

SCIE (2014) *Tenants who self-neglect* [online]. Available at: http://www.scie.org.uk/publications/guides/guide53/frontline-housing/self-neglect/ (accessed December 2017).

Tullis & Zangrillo (2013) Sexuality Education for Adolescents and Adults with Autism Spectrum Disorders. In *Psychology in the Schools* **50** (9) 866–875.

Valios N (2014) *Supreme Court ruling heralds sharp rise in Deprivation of Liberty Safeguards cases* [online]. Available at: http://www.communitycare.co.uk/2014/03/19/supreme-court-ruling-heralds-sharp-rise-deprivation-liberty-safeguards-cases/ (accessed December 2017).

Withers & Morris (2012) Sexual exploitation of people with intellectual disabilities. In: E Emerson, C Hatton, K Dickson R, Gone A, Caine & Bromley J (2012) *Clinical Psychology* (2nd Edn.) Chichester: Wiley.

Chapter 14:

Safeguarding adults with learning disabilities – what to do and how to prevent abuse

By Andy Mantell, Gill Concannon and Peter Warburton

Aims

- To highlight ways to stop abuse from happening.

- To understand the role of the quality of services in preventing the abuse of people with learning disabilities.

- To know what actions you should take if you become aware that abuse has occurred or is likely to take place.

Summary

This chapter considers the legislation and guidance on safeguarding adults. Drawing on case studies, it considers what can be done to prevent abuse and what you should do if you become aware that abuse has occurred or may take place. It should be read in conjunction with the previous chapter, 'Safeguarding adults with learning disabilities: what is abuse?'

Introduction

The Community Care Act (2014) introduced a statutory framework for the protection of adults from abuse. This replaced the previous *No Secrets* guidance (DoH, 2000) and is a radical change in how abuse of people with learning disability should be prevented and responded to. The emphasis has changed from a service-led, procedural response, concerned with investigation and protection, to a person-centred approach called *Making Safeguarding Personal* (LGA & ADASS, 2014). This places the person with a learning disability at the centre of shaping what should happen. It is a shift from a 'one size fits all' to a bespoke response.

Changing language, changing attitudes

The changes introduced by the Care Act (2014) and the accompanying *Care and Support Statutory Guidance* (DoH, 2017) are primarily a shift in approach and culture. This is reflected in a change in language. The table below highlights the key changes. One of the most important changes is that the person at risk or who has experienced abuse is no longer referred to as a vulnerable adult (although the term 'vulnerable' is still used in safeguarding children). This is because the term located the problem with the individual. It is not that a person has a learning disability which makes them vulnerable to abuse, rather it is a failing in their care and support or the actions of others.

Table 1: Changing terminology

Old term	New term	Implications
Safeguarding alert	Concern	Broader, less emotive
Investigating officer/manager	Enquiry officer/manager	Enquiry officer can be in any organisation, manager must be in local authority.
Vulnerable adult	Adult/adult at risk	Avoids pathologising the individual
Perpetrator/person alleged responsible	Alleged cause of risk	Less emotive, more nuanced name
Serious Case Reviews	Safeguarding Adult Reviews	Differentiated from Serious Case Reviews, which relate to children.

It is notable that there has been a shift in focus away from investigation (and its different levels) to enquiry, and that the language is less emotive, with people raising 'concerns' rather than 'alerts', and the term 'person or service thought to be the cause of risk' (abbreviated to 'cause of risk') replacing 'perpetrator'. While this new terminology may seem cumbersome, it reminds us that people who are the cause of risk may not fit neatly into our perception of perpetrators – they may, for example, be a carer who can no longer cope or perpetrators who have a learning disability.

What do we mean by safeguarding?

The Pan London Procedure defines safeguarding as 'protecting a person's right to live in safety, free from abuse and neglect' (ADASS, 2016). Safeguarding aims to stop, prevent or reduce the risk of harm, abuse or neglect by supporting adults in making choices and having control over their lives. It is also about being proactive and co-ordinating actions to prevent abuse of others being able to occur in the first place.

Anyone can experience an abusive situation, but Section 42 of The Care Act (2014) introduced a duty to those who are 18 or over who meet all three of the following criteria:

- An adult who has needs for care and support (whether or not any of those needs are being met).
- The adult may be experiencing, or is at risk of, abuse or neglect.
- As a result of their care and support needs, the adult is unable to protect themselves from either the risk of, or the experience of, abuse or neglect.

While local authorities have a specific duty to act, all organisations within that area have a responsibility to respond to and act to prevent abuse or neglect. Each local authority must have a Safeguarding Adults Board (SAB), which is made up of statutory partners from the local authority, clinical commissioning group and police, as well as non-statutory partners from local health and social care services, fire services, housing and voluntary sectors. The SAB's work includes drawing on single agency's experiences of adult safeguarding and uses these to support learning and service improvement. The SAB enables a forum for good interagency working as well as constructive inter-agency challenge and holds member organisations to account in a fair and transparent way. The SAB produces policies and procedures in each area to ensure that coherent and co-ordinated practices are followed to guarantee that adults are safeguarded in line with legislation and national guidance. The SAB also carries out Safeguarding Adult Reviews (SAR), in cases where a person dies or is seriously harmed. SAR's are about learning lessons, not about apportioning blame, and are designed to benefit and inform future practice.

Guiding principles for safeguarding practice

There are six principles to guide safeguarding practice, which can be remembered by the acronym 'EPPPPA':

Empowerment

The disability rights movement has a slogan, 'nothing about us without us', which encapsulates this key principle in safeguarding – it is about enabling people to have control over their lives. The individual's views should be sought and respected throughout, and even if they lack the mental capacity to make a decision (see below) they should be involved as much as possible. In such situations, or if they have substantial difficulty being involved in the enquiry process (see section 68 of the Care Act (2014)), an advocate should be involved to support them.

Prevention

Preventing abuse or neglect from occurring in the first place is far better than acting once it has occurred. Prevention encompasses building the individual's capacity for self-protection and improving the quality of their environment and network of support.

This can be about ensuring that the person with learning disabilities knows that the information they provide will be listened to and taken seriously. It can be about building their confidence to speak out and their ability to be assertive. This requires building their resilience and self-confidence by ensuring they have the information and support to make informed decisions.

Safeguarding is essential to promoting well-being, but promoting well-being also inhibits the cultures in which abuse can develop and thrive. Organisations that place the smooth running of the service above concerns for individual well-being can lead to short cuts being taken and depersonalising approaches becoming commonplace. In such environments, poor practice can become the norm and abusive practices go unchallenged. Good quality, person-centred care in health and social care services (whether, statutory , private, voluntary or not for profit) is one of the best ways to prevent abuse and neglect from being able to take place. However, where abuse occurs, then all organisations need to have clear procedures (compatible with the local multi-agency policy) to prevent harm.

Organisations must also cultivate learning rather than scapegoating cultures to ensure that the lessons from safeguarding and 'near misses' can be learnt. A near miss is where an incident occurs, which, while not significant enough to trigger a safeguarding concern, has the potential to become more serious in the future. For example, a member of staff is about to incorrectly use a hoist, but is corrected before they do so. This could be indicative of the need for better training and supervision. Near misses often remain unreported for fear of recrimination.

The Care Quality Commission has a responsibility for monitoring good quality services in health and social care. Their approach can be summarised by the 'mum test' – would you be happy with a loved one being cared for by this service? Wherever you work, always ask yourself that question. Quality services means having good management, staffing levels and training, but fundamentally it is also about having the right culture in the organisation and staff attitudes that never lose sight of those with whom they work.

Protection

The focus of protection under the Care Act (2014) has changed from being about services protecting vulnerable people to enabling people to protect themselves and make choices about what they want to happen.

Proportionate

At times it may be necessary to intervene in people's lives, for example where the person lacks the capacity to be able make decisions about what should happen. In such situations, there is a need to act but intervention must always be kept to the minimum. As Judge Munby (2010) remarked, 'What good is making someone safer if it just makes them miserable?'. This is in line with the Human Rights Act (1998), which also contains the principle of proportionality. Consequently, it is important to consider all the options. Be creative when identifying the solution and always try to use the least restrictive option.

Partnership

Collaborative working is essential. Local authorities must co-operate with each of their relevant partners and those partners must co-operate with the local authority. Agencies must have a commonly agreed policy to identify and assess risks. This requires shared policies on confidentiality and information sharing agreements that are based on the well-being of an adult at risk of abuse or neglect.

Accountability

Poor practices need to be stopped at the earliest opportunity. This requires open and transparent procedures in organisations. Lessons need to be learned from incidents, and provider services have a duty of candour, which is enforced by the Care Quality Commission (Health and Social Care Act (2014), Regulations 2014, Regulation 20). Workers' contracts of employment require them to be open and honest, but professionals have additional responsibilities under their professional codes of practice, for example, nurses are required to: 'Be open and candid with all service users about all aspects of care and treatment, including when mistakes or harm have taken place' (NMC, 2015:11).

Making safeguarding personal

The government has also introduced a new approach to safeguarding adults. In the past, a procedural 'one size fits all' approach was used, which tended to concentrate on organisations protecting the person and investigating with an aim of securing prosecutions. This procedural response focused on what actions the services took (outputs), rather than how the person is left feeling (outcomes). This can be summed up by the phrase 'hitting the target, but missing the point'. While the police still investigate and staff should ensure that forensic evidence is preserved, the new approach focuses much more upon what the person at risk would like to happen. It is a bespoke approach which seeks to give the individual control over what happens in their lives. Adopting a personal outcomes approach (Miller, 2012) can ensure that the individuals desired outcomes are identified and remain the focus of enquires.

Mental capacity

Point 1:1 of the statutory guidance on the Care Act (2014) states that 'the core purpose of adult care and support is to help people to achieve the outcomes that matter to them in their life' (DoH, 2017). Consequently, understanding a person's mental capacity and the best ways to enable them to participate fully in decisions are essential components of person-centred care planning. It is, however, in relation to safeguarding that professionals can struggle, when a person who appears to have capacity chooses to do an action that places them at risk (DoH, 2017).

Those who have substantial difficulty understanding the safeguarding process are entitled to an advocate. Anyone who lacks mental capacity also requires an Independent Mental Capacity Advocate to help them participate. Where a person lacks capacity then all the professionals involved will need to act in the service user's best interests. Mental incapacity should not be assumed or based upon a person's appearance. Mental capacity is assessed in relation to a particular issue, at a specific point in time (rather than being globally assessed). It is up to the person conducting the capacity assessment to prove lack of capacity, not for the person being assessed to prove anything.

There is a two-stage assessment:

Diagnostic test – Does the person have an impairment or disturbance in the functioning of their mind or brain, or is there some other sort of disturbance affecting the way their mind works?

and

Functional test – If so, does that impairment or disturbance mean that the person is **unable** to make a specific decision at the time it needs to be made?

The functional test consists of four criteria:

■ Does the person have a general understanding of what decision they need to make and why they need to make it?

■ Does the person have a general understanding of the likely consequences of making or not making the decision?

■ Is the person able to understand, retain, use and weigh up the information relevant to this decision?

■ Can the person communicate their decision?

This can be summarised as the URWC (Understand, Recall, Weigh-up and Communicate) test (Bennett, 2010).

The Mental Capacity Act (2005) introduced five principles, the first three help to guide the assessment of mental capacity and the last two focus on the support of a person who lacks mental capacity:

1. Assume capacity unless it is proved otherwise – this is to prevent, for example, people with learning disabilities from being assumed not to have capacity.

2. The right for people to be supported to make their own decisions – this is to ensure that the person is provided with the support they require in order to be able to make a decision.

3. Capacity does not always mean wisdom – this recognises that we do not always make wise decisions.

4. Any acts or decisions made on the person's behalf must be in their best interest – best interest is based on what the person would have wanted if they had capacity, taking into account their background, culture, religion etc., rather than what professionals may think is best for them.

5. Adopt the least restrictive intervention – this is similar to the proportionate principle, mentioned above. Actions should have the least restrictive impact upon a person's life to achieve what is required.

Case study: Jeremiah and Lucy

Lucy is 40 years old and has a moderate learning disability. She is a wheelchair user and lives in supported living with three other people. Her boyfriend, Jeremiah, is 44 years old and lives next door in similar accommodation. Jeremiah and Lucy have been overheard arguing, primarily about money, and name calling. Jeremiah appears to be having money troubles and is borrowing considerable amounts of money from Lucy. Some of her possessions have also gone missing, including her PlayStation and a hand-held computer device. Lucy has very little awareness of the value of money. She prefers coins to notes as she thinks they are worth more. When asked by support workers if Lucy is aware that Jeremiah borrows money from her, Lucy refuses to answer, saying only that she loves him except when he calls her names and takes her things.

Comment

It is essential to first determine Lucy's level of capacity and the best way to communicate and engage with her. From this, we can find out what she wants to happen and if there are any other concerns that she has which are not immediately apparent from the information we have been given. If Lucy has the capacity to give Jeremiah money, we still need to be mindful that she may be suffering from situational incapacity (see the previous chapter). We should also remember that the Mental Capacity Act (2005) advises that individuals are able to make 'unwise decisions' and ones that we would not always agree with.

There are several *potential* categories of abuse here:

1. Financial abuse by Jeremiah. If Jeremiah is taking Lucy's money without her knowledge, or forcing her to give him money, then that would also be theft and the police would need to be informed.

2. Domestic abuse by Jeremiah if he is controlling or coercing her. It appears that he is calling her names, which would be psychological and emotional abuse.

From the information provided, Lucy would appear to meet the criteria for a section 42 enquiry by social services, who should be contacted.

It would be very easy in this situation to view Lucy as the victim and Jeremiah as the perpetrator. However, this would deny Lucy the power to decide what she wants to do and may view Jeremiah simply as the problem. It is possible that Jeremiah is also experiencing financial abuse – is this why he has money problems? If this is the case, social services should be contacted so that a separate enquiry would need to be undertaken. This is one of the reasons why the less emotive language of 'person at risk' and 'cause of risk' has been adopted.

As far as Lucy is able, we should be working with her and Jeremiah to achieve the outcomes that Lucy wants. This might include someone becoming her Lasting Power of Attorney or her Deputy. They may both need some support about how to express themselves assertively, but in non-hurtful ways. A referral to the local Multi-agency Risk Assessment Conference (MARAC) (see previous chapter) may be necessary to ensure all agencies are aware and to ensure a plan has been agreed with Lucy to minimise risk.

Confidentiality

Professionals have a legal (Data Protection Act (1996), Human Rights Act (1998), Article 8 – right to respect for their private life) and ethical obligation to protect the confidentiality of information that service users and carers provide. Professionals must ensure service users are aware of how information they provide will be used and ensure they have choice in what happens to that information. In some circumstances, information such as safeguarding information may need to be shared even when the service user declines. There are three primary cases where this can happen:

1. Where other people may be at risk and information needs to be shared to protect them.

2. Where an offence has been committed, the police have to be notified.

3. When someone has breached their professional code of conduct, the appropriate professional body must be notified.

However, information should still only be shared on a need-to-know basis, in terms of who and how much information people are given. For instance, it may not be appropriate for all parties to receive details about someone's sexual activities, for example the parents of an adult with learning disabilities.

What should you do if you become aware that abuse may have occurred?

In order to become aware that abuse has or is occurring, vigilance is required. It is important to be receptive listeners so that people feel able to talk and divulge sensitive information.

Follow the organisation's safeguarding policy, noting that the police take the lead if a crime has been committed, and remember this check list:

- Take them seriously.
- Support the person/others to be safe.
- Get medical treatment if necessary.
- Call the police if in immediate danger.
- Use open questions e.g. 'tell, explain, describe' to gain an understanding of:
  - the situation
  - the adult's wishes
  - what actions may need to be taken, including raising a safeguarding concern.
- If they need support, then ensure they have the appropriate support or advocate.
- Know who to tell (follow the safeguarding policy).
- Preserve forensic evidence, for example damaged and soiled clothing.
- Share information appropriately.
- Record what has happened.

It is also important to avoid doing the following:

- Ignore, dismiss or joke about their concern.
- Assume someone else will do something.
- Speak to the person in a public place.
- Ask leading questions or begin to make enquiries inappropriately.
- Inform the cause of risk unless given the approval to do so where the police are involved.
- Contaminate or destroy evidence.

Case study: Cynthia

Cynthia is a 64-year-old woman who has a moderate learning disability. She was the only child still living with her parents when her mother died (her three elder sisters had left home by that point). Cynthia was always seen as being 'slow' at school. She was admitted to a long-stay hospital at the age of 30, following her mother's death. Cynthia moved into her own tenancy six years ago and receives daily support from an independent care provider. She has contact with one of her sisters, Margaret, who lives over a hundred miles away but telephones weekly.

Cynthia's workers have noticed that her behaviour has dramatically deteriorated and they have noticed a few unexplained bruises on her thighs and upper arms.

She is constantly hoarding food, and the workers have had to call in pest control to deal with mice because of this. Her sleep pattern is very poor, with neighbours reporting that they have seen her wandering along the street in her nightclothes. The police picked her up on one occasion and social workers had to be involved.

Cynthia is now incontinent on a daily basis. She has had a number of physical checks but no underlying cause could be found, and no attempt has been made to try to support her with her incontinence. Pads are being used and Cynthia's sister is concerned that this will lead to her being excluded from some activities, like swimming, which she previously enjoyed.

At a strategy meeting it emerged that most of the difficulties had started when Cynthia went to her exercise class. The manager of the provider organisation mentioned that Cynthia had become re-acquainted with Lucy who had been in hospital with her. Cynthia's sister said, 'Not her – she made Cynthia's life a misery!'

What types of abuse may be occurring?

Cynthia may be experiencing physical, psychological and emotional abuse from the person she does not like. The bruising and change in continence are also very concerning and could be indicative of sexual abuse. She is self-neglecting, but this may be made worse by organisational abuse from the carers – by not trying to help her manage her incontinence and in the general standard of her home they may be failing in their duty of care.

Key learning points

Preventing abuse is about being proactive to stop abuse being able to take place. Developing quality services, focused on the well-being of service users and having robust safeguarding procedures are the best way to inhibit abusive practices. Where abuse occurs, responses to prevent future abuse need to be person centred, to give the individual choice and control in what happens in their life. Mental capacity is a key component in decision making and requires that the practitioner do all they can to enable the person to participate, without assumptions and without undue influence from others.

References

Association of Directors of Adult Social Services (ADASS) (2016) *London Multi-agency Adult Safeguarding Policy* [online]. Available at: http://londonadass.org.uk/wp-content/uploads/2015/02/Pan-London-Updated-August-2016.pdf (accessed December 2017).

Bennett J (2010) Assessing Mental Capacity. *Social Care and Neurodisability* **1** (3) 44–48.

Department of Health (2000) *No Secrets: Guidance on developing and implementing multi-agency policies and procedures to protect vulnerable adults from abuse* [online]. Available at: www.gov.uk/government/uploads/system/uploads/attachment_data/file/194272/No_secrets__guidance_on_developing_and_implementing_multi-agency_policies_and_procedures_to_protect_vulnerable_adults_from_abuse.pdf (accessed February 2018).

Department of Health and Social Care (2017) *Care and Support Statutory Guidance* [online]. Available at: www.gov.uk/government/publications/care-act-statutory-guidance/care-and-support-statutory-guidance (accessed February 2018).

Local Government Association & The Association of Directors of Adult Social Services: *Making Safeguarding Personal: Guide 2014* [online]. Available at: www.local.gov.uk/sites/default/files/documents/Making%20Safeguarding%20Personal%20-%20Guide%202014.pdf (accessed February 2018).

Nursing and Midwifery Council (2015) *The Code: Professional standards of practice and behaviour for nurses and mid-wives* [online]. Available at: www.nmc.org.uk/glo.balassets/sitedocuments/nmc-publications/nmc-code.pdf (accessed February 2018).

Miller E (2012) *Individual Outcomes: Getting back to what matters*. Edinburgh: Dunedin.

Munby, Lord Justice (2010) 'What price dignity?', keynote address at LAG Community Care conference: *Protecting liberties*, London, 14 July.

Chapter 15:

Positive risk-taking – supporting people with learning disabilities to live a life like any other

By Kieron Beard, Barbara Barter and Annie Parris

Introduction

Historically, a risk-averse approach has dominated the lives of people with learning disabilities and their support structures. This has contributed to people with learning disabilities being denied the right to participate in the everyday activities from which we all learn and grow. In this chapter, we outline how a 'positive risk-taking' approach can be used throughout the risk assessment and management process to enable people with learning disabilities to live *A life like any other* (House of Lords & Joint Committee of Human Rights, 2008). We will briefly consider risk and why this is relevant in our work with people with learning disabilities. We will outline what we consider to be the key principles of 'positive risk-taking' and then attempt to provide a 'how to' guide for undertaking 'positive risk-taking' when working with people with learning disabilities. Finally, the challenges when implementing such an approach are considered and some potential solutions offered. Throughout, brief case studies are provided to highlight particular points of practice. The chapter is written from a practical perspective and is aimed at any worker who has a responsibility to assess, identify and manage risk in their roles supporting people with learning disabilities. Several questions are posed to aid the reader to reflect on current practice.

Aims

- To understand what is meant by the term 'positive risk-taking' and the reasons for advocating such an approach with people with learning disabilities.

- To appreciate where 'positive risk-taking' fits into the risk assessment and management process.

- To feel confident in undertaking a positive risk-taking approach in your work with people with learning disabilities.

What is risk?

Risk is an inherent part of life. Every choice we make and every action we take or don't take involves our exposure to a variety of risks. In common-sense terms, risk refers to the chance or possibility of being exposed to danger or harm. The Health & Safety Executive (2017) make a helpful distinction between hazards and risk, the former referring to anything that may cause harm and defining the latter as 'the chance, high or low, of someone being harmed by the hazard and how serious that harm could be'.

We are constantly assessing and managing risks as we go about our daily lives. For example, when we cross the road or get in the car to drive we assess the possible dangers. Much of this seems to occur automatically and within our heads and rarely do we ever document our risk assessments and management plans. To do so would leave little time for actually living our lives.

Our experience of risk is ever changing, with these experiences affecting our individual relationship to and perceptions of risk. These perceptions are coloured by the different opinions, values, beliefs and attitudes that we hold towards risk. For example, someone who has previously had a bad fall may view a walk on a mountain path as 'riskier' than someone who has never had that experience. An important point to note in difference to many people with learning disabilities, is that most of us will have the power to decide what risks we do and do not take in our lives.

Reflective question 1: Take a moment to think about what you value in life and some of the risks you may have taken in pursuit of this. Now think about how you may feel if others had the power to prevent you from taking those risks. In what ways may your life experience and choices differ?

Why is risk relevant in our work with people with learning disabilities?

Work with people with learning disabilities is governed by, and subject to, many laws and regulations:

- The Health & Social Care Act (2012)

- The Mental Capacity Act (2005)

- The Health and Safety at Work Act (1974)

- The Mental Health Act (1983; 2007)

- Care Quality Commission (CQC) regulations (Health and Social Care Act 2008 (Regulated Activities) Regulations 2014; Care Quality Commission (Registration) Regulations 2009)

- The Human Rights Act (1998)

- *Valuing People* (DoH, 2001)

- *Valuing People Now* (DoH, 2009)

If professionally qualified, the worker will likely have their own code of conduct and ethics to abide by. Regardless of our role, we all have a legal duty of care to protect the people that we support from harm. It is important to mention that this involves an inherent personal risk of being accused of negligence if it is found we have failed in this duty.

Historically, people with learning disabilities have been seen as a source of risk to themselves and others. The major risk management strategy to control these perceived risks was to segregate people with learning disabilities within large institutions away from wider society. Person-centred planning and other service philosophies that underpinned the closure of the long-stay hospitals and introduction of care in the community have long argued against the tendency towards risk aversion within learning disability services.

These historical perceptions of risk continue to be reflected in professional attitudes of both paternalism (the need to protect people with learning disabilities) and fear (the need to be protected from people with learning disabilities). This tendency towards risk aversion is reflected in the work of the Transforming Care Agenda (NHS England *et al*, 2017) that currently dominates the policy agenda in this area. This is attempting to shift the over-reliance on hospital settings to less restrictive and more rights-inclusive packages of support within the person's local community.

Like everyone else, risk will be present in the whole range of life experiences for people with learning disabilities, from their everyday choices and experiences such as going out, having relationships and taking part in meaningful activities to major life-changing decisions and events such as where and who to live with, whether to marry or have children. Supporting people with learning disabilities to manage risk in their lives is often a complex task. Many of the laws and regulations mentioned earlier can often conflict with each other, for example a common dilemma is trying to support someone's freedom to make choices while also ensuring this is done safely and protecting the person from harm. Another common example is a person with a learning disability wishing to go out alone, which may raise lots of worries about risk from family and supporters. In addition to these pressures, the current emphasis on public protection and fear of negative repercussions if things go wrong, means that supporters can err on the side of caution and over-estimate the level of risk in the lives of the people they support.

All of the above too often leads to people with learning disabilities experiencing a range of restrictive interventions and being denied the right to take the same risks as anybody else on an average day. It is important to think about the dangers or risks in choosing the safest option, as sometimes the safest option can be more detrimental than the original risk posed in terms of reducing the person's quality of life, level of independence and denying them access to basic human rights (see Chapter 2).

Case study: when a risk-averse approach makes the situation worse

'Olu' is a 28-year-old man with mild learning disabilities and autism and living in supported housing. Following his most recent annual health check he had been advised to try and lose some weight because he had put on 16lbs over the previous year and his body mass index (BMI) was now in the 'obese' range, increasing his risk of a range of health conditions. Olu's support team recognised that they had an important duty of care to support him in meeting his physical health needs but also feared they would be to blame if he developed a related physical health condition. They decided to support him to diet by restricting his portion size and access to sugary 'treats'. In response to this, Olu began to help himself to food, including some that belonged to his co-tenants. This led staff to place locks on the kitchen cupboards, further restricting access to food. By this point there were increasing incidents of Olu's staff team experiencing him as challenging. At his follow-up appointment with his nurse, Olu's weight remained the same as before.

Reflective question 2: If you supported the above person, how do you think you would have handled the situation? What do you think you would you have done the same or differently? Would you have made any additional considerations? Where would you have gone for support and guidance in this situation?

What is 'positive risk-taking'?

'Positive risk-taking' is an approach to risk assessment and management that focuses on achieving personal outcomes for people with learning disabilities through taking calculated and measured risks. It involves balancing the positive benefits gained from taking risks with the negative effects of not taking a risk. 'Positive risk-taking' is sometimes also called 'risk enablement', 'positive risk' or 'positive risk management'. It developed in response to the often paternalistic and risk averse cultures that tend to dominate within services.

'Positive risk-taking' reminds us that people have the right to live their lives to the fullest as long as this does not prevent others from doing the same. The biggest risk (especially to the person's rights and independence) may be in choosing the 'safest' option. However, it also reminds us of the need to support and respect the choices of people who opt for less risk-taking and independence in their lives.

Key principles of a 'positive risk-taking' approach

- **Working in collaboration with the people we support to assess and manage risk.** The risks that are most concerning to the people we support are not necessarily the same risks that concern us as supporters. Involving the people we support in risk decisions ensures we are focusing on the risks that matter most to them and can lead to increased accuracy of risk predictions. It requires the supporter to actively listen to the person's views and depends on trusting relationships between supporters and those supported. People with learning disabilities can be involved in a variety of ways; accessible materials and a supported decision-making model, for example, can help people to weigh up the pros and cons of their choices in a particular decision. Whitehead *et al* (2011) describe an example of a positive risk-taking process that is based on a 'human rights based approach' to risk assessment and management and the associated tools that have been developed to support user involvement and collaborative risk assessment.

- **Using the strengths and resources of the person, their support network and local community.** A strengths based approach encourages us to think about what can be achieved rather than what can't be achieved. Exploring a person's history, current situation and wishes for the future will reveal many qualities, abilities, capabilities, resources, wishes and desires that can be used in the weighing up of the pros and cons of the different options available. Using strengths and resources in this way also supports the person and their network to feel more confident in taking calculated risks. A PBS approach to support may help to identify strengths and resources, as well as areas for skills development along with identified approaches to support an individual to achieve their goals and wishes.

- **Shared decision-making.** In positive risk-taking, risk decisions should never be the responsibility of one person as this can increase the fear of responsibility and blame if things go wrong and leads to more risk-averse decisions being made. Risk decisions should involve the person and their support network as a variety of perspectives can also help open up new possibilities. The likely outcome is that more balanced decisions are made that respect the positive potential and desired outcomes for the person supported.

- **Planned and structured.** Positive risk-taking takes a structured approach in order to support someone to take calculated and managed risks in pursuit of their goals. It involves breaking an activity or task down into small, calculated risks and considering what is needed to support the person to achieve their goal safely.

- **Defending our decisions instead of taking defensive actions.** Positive risk-taking recognises that risk can never be eliminated, only minimised, and despite the best made plans sometimes things can and do go wrong. If it is clearly documented that all possible outcomes (both negative and positive) of each choice/risk area have been considered, and efforts have been made to manage the risk in a proportionate way, then it is much more likely that supporters will find themselves on the right side of the law. An exception to this is when the person has been assessed as not having capacity to make a particular decision as laid out in the Mental Capacity Act (2005). In such circumstances a 'best interest' process must be followed that aims to make a specific decision involving the person with a learning disability and their network

When to undertake a positive risk-taking approach?

This approach to risk should form an integral part of the support planning and risk assessment and review process to enhance rather than restrict the person with learning disabilities. However, it has particular value in situations when new activities or experiences are being considered or when the person being supported has few choices and limited opportunities to take risks. Positive risk taking may form an integral part of a PBS or care plan.

Who to include in the positive risk-taking process?

The most important person to involve is the person being supported. There may be occasions when the person's involvement is limited, such as if the person refuses to engage in the process or if they require a high level of support to communicate their needs or wishes. However, it is still important to seek to try and understand the person's wishes and feelings on the subject. This understanding may come from what you or others already know about the person, their life history and experiences and how they have reacted in similar circumstances in the past. It is generally helpful to involve as many people from the person's support network and local community as possible, provided the person being supported consents to their involvement. It is also important to be mindful that some people involved in the positive risk-taking process may hold beliefs that the person needs to be protected and cared for at the expense of taking calculated risks. Therefore, the more people involved the more diverse perspectives there are from which to draw when attempting to balance any risks.

Positive risk assessment

The amount of time, effort and resources that goes into the risk assessment process will depend on many factors, such as the role of the supporter and the policies/procedures of the employing organisation. The guiding factor should be how able the person with learning disabilities is to reasonably predict and manage risk in their lives, how likely the particular outcome will be and how serious the outcome would be if it was to occur. For any risk assessment to be meaningful it needs to be an ongoing process where new experiences are learnt from. Additionally, it may be helpful to consider the following:

- Risk is a two-way process – what are the risks to and from the person (these can include risks to and from themselves, others and the environment).

- Risk assessment is based on good quality information – information about the person, their support network and the proposed choice or activity.

- A helpful starting point can be to meet with the person and their support network (both formal and informal supporters) and explore the person's strengths, abilities, weaknesses and particular areas of vulnerability. What is the evidence from the person's history of actual risk rather than perceived risk?

- Define the nature of the risk involved in any given choice (who is at risk, what is the frequency and level of risk, what are the possible short-term and long-term, positive and negative outcomes).

- At each stage think about and discuss together – how can we increase freedom and choice in this situation while keeping the risk at an acceptable level. What is considered an acceptable level is a value judgement that will depend on the individual characteristics of the person with learning disabilities and their support network. However, it can be helpful to consider whether this level of risk would be acceptable to yourself or a member of your family.

Positive risk management plans

The purpose of a risk management plan is to enable a balance to be struck between enabling as much freedom and choice as possible for the person, while also ensuring that the potential negative consequences of the risk are appropriately managed and controlled. There can be a need for creativity in devising risk management plans, involving the person and their support network as much as possible and also considering how their strengths and resources can be drawn on to manage any potential risks. This is often referred to as 'not using a sledge hammer to crack a nut' – any actions taken to manage the potential risk should be necessary and proportionate to the level of risk posed, and that any strategies employed should be those least restrictive of the person's individual rights, freedom and choices. The risk management plan needs to be communicated to all those involved and there needs to be a process for monitoring the outcomes with a time set aside in the future to review the risk formally. The case study below provides a follow-up to Olu's situation described in the first case study, as an example of a positive risk-taking approach for a specific risk area.

Case study: supporting positive risk-taking
Brief outline of risk decision to be made

Olu has been advised by his nurse that it would be beneficial to lose weight. Olu agrees with this but thinks it is more important to improve his fitness and would like to join the local community gym. In Olu's care notes it is documented that when Olu previously attended a gym a number of years ago there was an incident that resorted in Olu being excluded from the gym for damaging a machine. Olu's support team are reluctant to support him to the gym and instead have focused on controlling his calorie intake.

How was the person involved in this risk decision? (Is there any evidence that they may lack capacity to make this decision?)

- Undertook collaborative, rights-based risk assessment with learning disability nurse and support of advocate.
- No evidence to indicate lack of capacity to make this risk decision.
- Attended risk enablement meeting.

Who else was consulted?

- Support team, particularly key-worker.
- Parents.
- Siblings.
- Behaviour Support Specialist devising Positive Behaviour Support Plan.
- LD Nurse.
- Gym instructor.

What personal outcome does the person want to achieve?

- Improve health and fitness (this is more important to Olu than losing weight).
- Lose then maintain a healthy weight.
- Increase self-esteem and confidence.

What choices does the person have to achieve this? (Please include the possible negative impact of doing nothing and avoiding the risk all together.)

■ Strict diet that Olu controls.
■ Strict diet that the support team control.
■ Focus on exercise and join the local gym.
■ Focus on exercise but exercise at home.
■ Mixture of all the above.
■ Do nothing (continue as we are).

What are the possible risks and benefits of each choice (and to whom)?

Choice	Possible risks	Possible benefits
Strict diet that Olu controls.	May cause him stress and be ineffective.	Less conflict with staff. Sense of personal achievement.
Strict diet that support team control.	Increasing conflict with staff and restrictive environment at home.	Less for Olu to manage. Once the choice is taken away he may adapt and accept.
Focus on exercise and join the local gym.	May be incidence of behaviour that can challenge that may result in Olu's exclusion from the gym.	Olu would like to do this. Ordinary community activity. Opportunity to increase social presence and develop informal supports.
Focus on exercise but exercise at home.	Not able to learn from others. Restricted to home environment. May get in the way of co-tenants.	Opportunity to exercise.

Choice	Possible risks	Possible benefits
Mixture of all the above.	Same risks as outlined above.	Opportunity to exercise and control calorie intake most likely to support Olu to meet his goals. Access to community.
Do nothing (continue as we are).	Increasing episodes of behaviour that challenges and conflict with staff. Increasing restrictions.	Staff feel they are doing the right thing.

For which choices do the possible benefits outweigh the possible risks (please state)?

Olu being in control of his own diet and exercising at home appears to be the most obvious solution. However, there are many potential benefits to Olu joining the community gym if the risk of him engaging in behaviour that can challenge is minimised.

What strengths and resources exist for the person and their network that can be drawn on to help manage the associated risks?

■ One of Olu's support team also has a keen interest in health and fitness.

■ Olu is currently working with a behaviour support specialist and has a Positive Behaviour Support Plan with proactive and reactive strategies for supporting him with his behaviours that can challenge.

What steps can be taken to control and manage the associated risks?

■ Consult Positive Behaviour Support Plan – strategies may be adaptable to the gym setting.

■ Olu could attend initially to meet with the gym instructor and his support worker who is most interested in order to understand what behaviour is expected of him.

■ They could then visit at a less busy time.

■ The previous incident involved Olu refusing to leave a running machine and becoming increasingly agitated – a social story could support him to use this machine last when he has already expended some energy and for a set period of time with a definite ending (using auto-programme on the machine).

If our worst fears do come true, how will we handle this? (Crisis? Contingency plans?)

■ Contingency plan (trying to prevent feared outcome) – see above and strategies in Positive Behaviour Support Plan.

■ Crisis plan (how to handle feared outcome) – 2:1 support for first week of visits then review. Use of on-call system if additional staff required to support. Follow reactive PBS plan. Complete incident and ABC to try and understand and learn from incident.

What support is required for the staff team if things go wrong?

■ Incident de-brief with support team.

Is this level of risk considered acceptable to the person and their network? (Record any objections and further discussions.)

■ Yes, except two members of support team. Initially agreed they won't support him with this activity until supported to feel more confident.

Who has this positive risk-taking plan been communicated to?

■ Olu
■ Support team
■ Behaviour support specialist
■ Social worker
■ LD nurse
■ Parents
■ Gym instructor

What is the plan for reviewing this risk-taking plan?

■ Review following each visit for first two weeks.
■ Review following any significant incidents or near misses.
■ Review if the situation or staff changes, or at a minimum every six-months.

Reflective question 3: Compare and contrast the response in this case study with your response to reflective question 2. Does anything surprise you? Is there anything missing from either your thinking or the response in the case study? Now try to consider how it would feel from Olu's perspective.

Some challenges and solutions

As stated earlier, supporting people with learning disabilities to take risks can be a complex and challenging process. When implementing a positive risk-taking approach a number of challenges can arise that, if not accounted for, can have a negative impact on the quality of life for the person with learning disabilities and deprive them of their basic human rights and opportunities to learn and grow as a person. Some of these challenges will now be considered, along with potential solutions.

- **Working in a risk-averse culture –** To manage the fear of negative consequences and potential repercussions to the worker if things do go wrong, it is important that they feel supported by their employing organisation and partner agencies to engage in a positive risk-taking approach. Any organisation that expects its staff to undertake this approach should provide a positive risk-taking policy that makes the values and rationale underlying this approach explicit and provides guidance and direction that is supportive of positive risk-taking. Individual fears and concerns can be proactively explored through support structures that are already in place, such as supervision. When things don't go as planned it is also important that the worker feels supported in learning from the incident and local procedures such as post-incident support should be available.

- **Risk assessment forms –** Many organisations have their own risk assessment forms that are required to be filled in. This runs the risk of being seen as a tick-box exercise and presents a barrier to the meaningful consideration of risk in a given situation for an individual with learning disabilities. While it is important that any required documentation is completed, the risk assessment form should not dominate the conversations concerning risk and the ideas presented in this chapter could help supplement any areas that are covered by an individual risk assessment form.

- **Working with a lack of resources –** The resources available to enable positive risk-taking will have an impact on what steps can be taken to manage or control a perceived risk. Again, creativity and 'thinking outside the box' can be valuable here. If funded or statutory support is lacking, then utilising and sometimes building in natural supports, such as friends, family and members of the local community, can go a long way in realising the benefits of 'positive risk-taking'.

- **Particularly challenging or complex risk areas –** Supporting people with learning disabilities to take and manage everyday risks can present some challenges. However, there are particular risk areas that are likely to present many complex or challenging dilemmas to be thought through. Supporting someone with their sexual identity, for example, can involve many taboo beliefs and attitudes regarding sex and relationships for people with learning disabilities that can adversely affect how risk is perceived and worked with. Many people with learning disabilities who require support can also engage in behaviours that others find challenging or also suffer with their mental health. It is important to seek professional support at these times through the local multi-disciplinary team (MDT) where specialist advice and access to structured, evidence-based risk assessment tools can be used to inform a positive risk-taking approach.

Summary

People with learning disabilities have the same right to make choices and take risks in their lives as anybody else. Not all risk is bad and we need to take risks to grow and learn. However, all too often, because of pressures in the system and individual risk perceptions and attitudes, people with learning disabilities are denied these basic rights and choices with overwhelmingly negative consequences for their quality of life. It is important to remember that sometimes the biggest danger is in *not* taking a calculated risk. Positive risk-taking has developed as a means to overcome this tendency towards risk aversion and allow a balance to be achieved between the individual's freedom and safety. It is about maximising the benefits of taking a risk while also controlling for any potential negative consequences in the service of supporting people with learning disabilities to achieve their own personal outcomes and live a life like any other.

References

Department of Health (2001) *Valuing People: A new strategy for Learning Disability for the 21st Century* [online]. Available at: https://www.gov.uk/government/publications/valuing-people-a-new-strategy-for-learning-disability-for-the-21st-century (accessed December 2017).

Department of Health (2009). *Valuing People Now: A new three-year strategy for people with learning disabilities* [online]. Available at: http://webarchive.nationalarchives.gov.uk/20130105063552/http://www.dh.gov.uk/en/Publicationsandstatistics/Publications/PublicationsPolicyAndGuidance/DH_093377 (accessed December 2017).

Health and Safety Executive (2017) Available at: http://www.hse.gov.uk/ (accessed December 2017).

House of Lords & House of Commons Joint Committee on Human Rights (2008) *A Life Like any Other? Human Rights of adults with learning disabilities* [online]. Available at: https://publications.parliament.uk/pa/jt200708/jtselect/jtrights/40/40i.pdf (accessed December 2017).

NHS England, the Association of Adult Social Services (ADASS), the Care Quality Commission (CQC), Local Government Association (LGA), Health Education England (HEE) and the Department of Health (DH). Transforming Care (Online). Available at: https://www.england.nhs.uk/learning-disabilities/care/ (Accessed: 20 August 2017).

Whitehead R, Carney G & Greenhill B (2011) Encouraging positive risk management: Supporting decisions by People with Learning Disabilities using a Human Rights-Based Approach. In: Whittington R and Logan C (Eds) *Self-Harm and Violence: Towards best practice in managing risk in mental health services*. Oxford: John Wiley & Sons, pp215–236.

Chapter 16:

Hate crime – crime against disabled people

By Christine Koulla-Burke, Marian Jennings & Eddie Chaplin

Aims

- To have an understanding of the different types of hate crime and how common it is.

- To have an insight in to how hate crime affects people with learning disabilities using scenarios and real-life cases.

- To look at strategies to reduce the risk of being a victim of hate crime.

Summary

Hate crime is directed at certain groups in society because of their perceived differences. When hate crime occurs it can be dehumanising and pushes people further towards the outer boundaries of society. Hate crime against people with learning disabilities can be more problematic to gauge due to a number of factors such as difficulties in reporting and people's concerns and experiences not being taken seriously. This chapter uses case studies and information from reports to offer a brief insight into hate crime and strategies people with learning disabilities might use to minimise the risk of becoming a victim.

Introduction

The term 'hate crime' focuses on the crime and the motivation for it. However there is often criticism that it is not explicit about what group is the target. Another term in use is 'crimes against disabled people', which is used by the Crown Prosecution Service as it focuses more on the victim. The term 'hate crime' will be used where appropriate so as not to confuse readers. The term also extends to a number of other groups who are victims but not necessarily seen as having a disability, such as crimes motivated by race or religion. Hate crime, however, is not the only term coming under question. The term 'mate crime' has also had its critics. Mate crime has been consistently used as it relates to people with learning disabilities being 'befriended' and abused by people who might be seen as friends to outsiders. The term mate crime has been criticised for making it more palatable and diminishes the cruelty and intent that is found in the huge number of cases where abuse is perpetrated by someone close to the victim. There is a difference in how the law responds to so called 'mate crime' and 'grooming'. The term does not reflect the seriousness of the crime and should not be used. In reality, perpetrators are grooming vulnerable individuals and using the fact that they are lonely and desperate for friendship as an opportunity to abuse them. The Independent Police Complaints Commission published its review into the Pilkington case in May 2011, and in September 2011 the Equality and Human Rights Commission (EHRC) published its inquiry into disability related harassment, *Hidden in Plain Sight*, which made recommendations on this issue.

Agencies find it difficult to describe many incidents as hate crime because many of them are not motivated by hate, however its impact is cruel, manipulative and abusive to someone's personal liberty and dignity. Disability hate crime would describe the motivation of the perpetrator more realistically and afford the victim the seriousness of the crime against them.

Approximately 15% of adults worldwide have a disability (Hughes *et al*, 2012) and between 1-3% have a learning disability. In recent years there has been an increase in public awareness around hate crime. Hate crime describes an incident against another person designed to cause them harm which is carried out due to prejudice or hate. Hate crimes can happen to someone because they are different or perceived as differed. So, if someone has a learning disability or their attacker believes they have a learning disability, and that motivates the attack or incident, it is considered a hate crime.

Violence and hostility is a daily experience for some people with disabilities. The Equality and Human Rights Commission (2009) and evidence suggests that this is the case also for people with learning disabilities. *Living in Fear* (Mencap, 2000; Beadle-Brown *et al*, 2014) reported that 88% of people with a learning disability had experienced bullying or harassment in the past year, with 73% in a public place, and 23% had been physically assaulted. Sometimes these are referred to as hate incidents and they may or may not be regarded as hate crimes but still will cause considerable stress to the person. It is estimated that approximately only 3% of incidents are recorded by the police. These can range from the most serious of crimes to minor incidents of bullying and harassment and can include both verbal and physical assaults.

Verbal assaults

- name-calling
- offensive jokes
- threatening violence
- threatening phone calls or text messages
- hate mail
- internet abuse.

Physical assaults

- physical attacks
- damage to a person's home or possessions
- criminal damage
- harassment
- murder
- sexual assault
- theft
- fraud
- burglary
- hate mail
- causing distress
- arson.

The experiences of people with learning disabilities are wide and varied. Many live in the community leading independent valued lives. Many experience harassment, abuse or related crime and this is mainly in the community. The main perpetrators reported by people with learning disabilities are neighbours and school children. One report, which focused on the experiences of 67 people with learning disabilities who had been the victims of crime (Gravel, 2012), found the following.

Locations of incidents	Types of incidents	Types of perpetrators
■ Within the home – 29% ■ Outside (e.g. parks, shopping areas, on the street) – 28% ■ Around the home – 27% ■ At work – 5% ■ Public transport – 4% ■ Pubs or restaurants – 4% ■ Supported housing – 3%	■ Name calling, ridiculing, verbal abuse – 27% ■ Attacks on property, uninvited entry, burglary, destroying possessions – 23% ■ Borrowing/stealing money, being made to buy things – 20% ■ Physical abuse, assaults, threats – 18% ■ Taking emotional advantage of people – 6% ■ Sexual abuse, assault, rape – 4% ■ Accusations of abuse, trying to get interviewers in trouble – 2%	■ Neighbours/known people living locally – 25% ■ School children or young people – 17% ■ Predatory 'friends' –13% ■ Strangers in the street – 11% ■ Family members (siblings, children, uncles, aunts) – 7% ■ Unknown – 6% ■ Work colleagues – 5% ■ Care or support workers – 4%

(Gravel, 2012)

Reducing the risk of hate crime

The following case studies illustrate some of the issues faced by people with learning disabilities who experience hate crime, and each is followed by information as to how we might reduce the risks of these crimes taking place.

Case study: John

John feels highly anxious when he is out and about when school children are out from school. He describes feeling scared and very sad by the things they call him. John had to be referred to a counsellor that was able to help him manage his anxiety but this did not challenge the perpetrators.

We need to recognise the need for preventative measures and the importance of educating children to teach them respect for others and respect for difference, creating not only compassion, but empathy, to ensure that attitudes are changed. However, we cannot underestimate the power or peer influence. The solution can be found in peer education and whole-school approaches that can challenge from within the behaviour of their students. The onus should not be on the victims to stay hidden and out of the path of school children; there is a need for a legal solution that can support whole-school approaches.

In terms of 'mate crime', it is important to highlight the issue of loneliness. Young and old report feeling lonely, which is often an ideal opportunity for perpetrators to take advantage of this need for friendship.

Case study: Pete

Pete inherited some money from his parents and got befriended by his neighbour, who was always around and eating out of Pete's fridge. Pete saw him as a good friend and confided in him. It was hard to believe that Pete saw nothing wrong with his neighbour borrowing money until there was no more inheritance. When Pete was stuck for cash he asked for some of the money back only to get the response, 'What money? You gave me that money and never said I had to pay it back'. Pete was supported to seek advice but in the end decided that he would not pursue the matter in court as he was afraid of his neighbour.

Building environments that promote whole-community approaches that include people in their neighbourhoods and communities will help keep them safe. Inclusive practice and community connecting brings people into the lives of vulnerable adults and ultimately they will be included, with many keeping an eye out for their safety and well-being. (For more information, see www.mentalhealth.org.uk/learning-disabilities/our-work/family-friends-community/community-connecting.) Furthermore, developing circles of friends will offer individuals the opportunity to become independent and more in control of their lives. These circles will also make sure that the individual is leading a valued lifestyle in the community. For more information, see Burke (2006).

Case study: Jane

Jane told her circle of friends that she was afraid when at home. She lived with three other people in supported housing. Her friends enquired at the house to ascertain why Jane was afraid of the person in the next room and she was asked if the person had hurt her. The response was that, yes, she had been attacked by her house mate and had required hospitalisation, but they were in separate rooms and they were never alone together. Jane's friends pursued this and had Jane moved to another house. This was not easy to do, and at no stage did anyone find it strange that Jane continued to live somewhere where she had been seriously assaulted by someone in the next room. Had this been any other citizen or non-disabled individual this would have been seen as an assault and unacceptable.

Developing social capital by building people's networks and creating civic mindedness is one model of prevention. The other factors that need consideration are those based on equality of access and prevention of discrimination. As well as the whole criminal justice system, the nature of support they offer victims and witnesses, the way they investigate and prosecute perpetrators. Failures within the criminal justice system to respond to crimes against disabled people are well reported, and people with learning disabilities feel that there is no point in reporting a crime because they will not be believed by the police. A lot needs to be done to improve the prosecution of crimes against disabled people. The changing terminology goes a long way in moving the focus of the debate away from 'hate' and 'mate' to 'crimes against disabled people' and grooming, which will help create a culture that views these acts as criminal, rather than as petty issues or squabbles.

Equality under the law should be undisputed and there is still a long way to go to ensure that people with learning disabilities are protected by the legal system. This includes challenging what can only be described as 'institutional disablism' (sic), and while there has been progress in relation to certain crimes, there is still a lack of confidence in the speed of change.

And much needs to change. There needs to be a means for flagging that someone has a learning disability that is consistent and that can be tracked across the system in order to be able to confidently retrieve information on the state of crimes against a person with learning disabilities. Police need to be trained to know how best to interview and support a person with learning disabilities when they have been the victim of a crime, and this training needs to be mandatory rather than left to voluntary organisations. A clear recommendation from public reports is that all police, CPS and victim support staff need to be fully aware of the statutory responsibilities as listed in the section 146 of the Criminal Justice Act (2003) and there needs to be a common policy definition that is universally recognised and applied at all levels, from the bottom up. This needs to be accessible to everyone without being open to misinterpretation. This is reinforced in the Joint Disability Hate Crime Review, 2013. Progress needs to be recorded and an evidence base established, with an onus on academics to create a body of literature that enhances our understanding of the nature of this type of crime, which is currently so misunderstood that it leads to gross discrimination.

Another area in need of change is that of the underreporting of crime, which is a significant concern and needs to be researched and supported (Chaplin & Mukhopadhyay, 2018; Breton, 2013). We need to see more joined-up and consistent initiatives by the CPS and the police, and we need community engagement projects that better inform and support. These initiatives need to better train those that support people with learning disabilities to understand and recognise when someone is reporting a crime or is being groomed. Victim Support have an important role to play and it should be flagged up that reasonable adjustments will be needed in response to reports of a crime.

Support therefore needs to be offered following a crime, but for those who have not been a victim it is as important to help them understand what they can do to make themselves less vulnerable to future crimes. It may also be necessary for those supporting an individual to find support and information themselves so they can help educate the people in their care to be aware of any potential risks (see the real life case studies on p198).

It is useful to look carefully at situations in which a person may be particularly vulnerable and, if there is a risk, consider what changes can be made or what support offered to reduce the risk. For example, a person might go out at different times of the day when there are fewer people about, or when there is less chance of school children being on a bus who might tease or harass them (of course, this is on top of wider steps that need to be taken to educate the schoolchildren, as discussed earlier). Another example might be a person with a learning disability getting pestered in the street for money, which might be prevented if the person is encouraged to use different routes when they are out and about. Of course, it is unfortunate that changes to a person's routine like these need to be made at all, but if it can help protect them or make them less anxious, then these steps need to be considered.

Some people are targeted in their own homes where they are thought to be a soft target, and so it is important to review basic home security such as locks and bolts, panic alarms or even closed circuit television (CCTV). Some people may suffer from frequent low-level abuse, which taken as isolated incidents appears fairly insignificant. If this is the case, it is a good idea to keep a record that can then be used by the police or as evidence should a future case come to court.

However, learning to handle and respond to these difficult situations, rather than simply avoiding them, is more helpful in the long term. This can be done by role playing potentially difficult scenarios until the person is confident that they can use new skills in real situations, such as saying no to requests for money. It is important to get a balance and to know, just like everyone else, when it may be better to avoid a situation and when to tackle it more proactively, which can be a more difficult skill to master.

While changes in routine and behaviour to reduce the threat of falling victim to a crime can be effective, this can have a considerable impact on their freedom and choice. Until hate crime is tackled and more is done to support people, the practice of restricting movements and living in fear will continue. Part of the role of supporting people is to know more about their lives and when they feel vulnerable. People with learning disabilities will often not be heard when they say they are being pestered for money, being made fun of in the street or even when made to do things they don't want to do. For some there needs to be greater communication within circles of support to assist them, while others just need to be listened to and have it recognised that there is a problem. Once we know someone is experiencing hate crime, practical steps can be taken.

Acknowledge that it can sometimes feel like it will never end but reassure the person that there are some things that can be done to make it stop, and make sure the person knows they are not alone. Implement some of the changes suggested previously and check that the strategies have worked by asking the person to fill in a diary.

To end the chapter we will look at real life cases that portray the stark reality of the cruelty and brutality of hate crime.

Real life case studies

Tuesday's Friends – The case of Steven Hoskins

Steven's case made the news in 2006. Steven lived in Cornwall and had a mild to moderate learning disability. Steven was a victim of 'mate crime'. The protagonists in Steven's case were known as his 'Tuesday Friends' – Tuesday was the day that Steven collected his benefits. For over a year Steven was systematically abused. His money was stolen, he was treated as a slave and he was beaten. And yet Steven believed that the perpetrators of these crimes were his friends.

These 'friends' moved into Steven's flat and began using it as a venue for selling drugs. For their amusement, they would lead Steven around the flat on a dog lead and force him to call them 'sir' and 'madam'.

On the 5th July 2006, three members of the gang tortured Steven until he falsely confessed to being a paedophile. Steven was then taken to a viaduct in St Austell. Once at the viaduct, he was forced over the safety rail and he fell to his death.

Steven's three killers were jailed for over 40 years.

Both Steven and his killers were known to the police and social services. Steven was known to be a person at risk. In the months before his death, Steven had made 2 calls to a variety of agencies in which he mentioned that threats had been made against him. Police and social service visited Steven's flat on several occasions but did not pick up on the fact that he was being abused. All the agencies involved in

1Steven's support were aware that he cancelled his care a month before he died. No one thought to question the reasons behind the cancellation. The serious case review into Steven's death found that there were over 40 missed opportunities to intervene in his situation.

David Askew

David was a 64-year-old man with a severe learning disability. In the six years before his death in 2010, David and his family had reported instances of targeted antisocial behaviour on over 80 occasions to the Greater Manchester Police Force.

David collapsed and died in his front garden after confronting a group of youths who were attempting to vandalise his property. After his death it was revealed that the whole family had suffered years of abuse from generations of local youths. David had been a particular target.

The Independent Police Commission's report into David's death found that although individual local police officers had tried to help the family, there had been significant gaps in communication between services and in the recording of incidents. David had not been recognised as an adult at risk. The local council, NHS staff and the Housing Association who owned David's house were also criticised for viewing David as a problem rather than looking at him as a victim of a campaign of hate.

Fiona Pilkington and Francesca Harwick

In October 2007, Fiona Pilkington killed herself and her daughter, Francesca, who had a severe learning disability, by setting fire to the car in which they were sitting. For several years Fiona, Francesca and Francesca's brother Anthony had been subjected to constant abuse from local youths in their neighbourhood. As a result, the family were virtual prisoners in their own home. Fiona had contacted the police on more than 30 occasions to report the abuse and concerns had also been raised by Fiona's mother, by neighbours, and by their local MP.

The Independent Police Commission found that the police had underestimated the emotional trauma of constant harassment. The report also focused on the failure of the police and other agencies to identify the family as being at risk. Concerns were also raised about the fact that the family were not identified as victims of hate crime even though Francesca and Anthony had been specifically targeted because of their disabilities.

Summary and conclusion

In summary, there are many changes required in order to empower people with learning disabilities to lead full, inclusive lives in the community and to prevent loneliness and the vulnerabilities that this can bring. Building an agenda of empowerment is crucial if we are to support change. The more that people are seen and live inclusive lifestyles the safer they will be. It is vital to strengthen relationships that are based on true friendship, and to understand the behaviours of those that are not friends, but who exploit, abuse and groom these vulnerable people. Supporting people to better understand crimes against disabled people, what it means, and how they can assert their rights as equal citizens is also essential. We need to support not only their emotional resilience but also their self-esteem and confidence, as those who are targeted are particularly vulnerable and often without adequate support, which can have a serious impact on their mental well-being and increase the risk of mental ill-health and behavioural problems, which will have a negative impact on their quality of life.

References

Beadle-Brown J, Richardson L, Guest C, Malovic, A, Bradshaw J & Himmerich J (2014) *Living in Fear: Better outcomes for people with learning disabilities and autism*. Tizard Centre, University of Kent, Canterbury.

Brereton S (2013) Living in a different world: joint review of disability hate crime. *Probation Journal* **60** (3) pp345–6.

Burke C (2006) *Building Community Through Circles of Friends: A practical guide to making inclusion a reality for people with learning disabilities*. London: Foundation for People with Learning Disabilities.

Chaplin E & Mukhopadhyay (2018) Autism spectrum disorder and hate crime. *Advances in Autism* **4** (1) pp30–36, https://doi.org/10.1108/AIA-08-2017-0015

Equality and Human Rights Commission (2009) *Research Report 21: Disabled people's experiences of targeted violence and hostility* [online]. Available at: https://www.equalityhumanrights.com/sites/default/files/research_report_21_disabled_people_s_experiences_of_targeted_violence_and_hostility.pdf (accessed March 2018).

Equality and Human Rights Commission (2011) *Hidden in Plain Sight: Inquiry into disability-related Harassment* [online]. Available at: https://www.equalityhumanrights.com/sites/default/files/ehrc_hidden_in_plain_sight_3.pdf (accessed March 2018).

Gravell C (2012) *Loneliness and Cruelty: People with learning disabilities and their experiences of harassment, abuse and related crime in the community*. London: Lemos & Crane.

Hughes K, Bellis MA, Jones L, Wood S, McCoy E, Eckley L, Bates G, Mikton C, Shakespeare T & Officer A (2012) Prevalence and risk of violence against adults with disabilities: a systematic review and meta-analysis of observational studies. *The Lancet* **379** (9826) pp1621–9.

MENCAP (2000) *Living in Fear: Better outcomes for people with learning disabilities and autism* [online]. Available at: http://www.mcch.org.uk/pages/multimedia/db_document.document?id=8009 (accessed March 2018).

Chapter 17:

People with learning disabilities in the Criminal Justice System

By Eddie Chaplin & Karina Marshall-Tate

Summary

Historically, people with a low IQ have been known to commit crimes at higher rates than the rest of the population. Although there is robust evidence linking intelligence to crime, it is unclear how this might apply to people with learning disabilities. In this chapter we examine the evidence around offending and people with learning disability, what is currently being done to help this group, and how to support someone through the CJS.

Introduction

Over time, a robust link between intelligence and crime has been established, and although there is a disproportionate number of people with learning disability in the Criminal Justice System (CJS), there is little evidence to suggest that people with learning disability are more at risk of offending. The reasons for this are unclear but may include social naivety and misinterpretations of their behaviour as offending, or they may be under peer-pressure to undertake criminal acts in order to maintain friendships.

The relationship between learning disabilities, mental illness and offending

Evidence

People with learning disabilities are more likely to experience mental health problems than the general population, and mental illness – along with substance misuse that often comes with mental ill-health – might increase the likelihood of offending, as might factors such as poverty, unemployment and other socio-economic considerations. Whether people with a learning disability and mental illness have higher rates of offending than people with learning disability alone is not clear.

We know that rates of mental health problems in the prison population are higher than the rest of the population (McCarthy, 2016), but we do not know if these mental health issues existed at the time the offences took place or if they have come about as a result of incarceration.

In terms of specific mental illnesses, the links between positive psychotic symptoms, such as hallucinations and delusions, and offending behaviour can often be overstated and they continue to be put forward as an explanation in some cases.

Role of positive symptoms	Rationale
An individual acting upon a false belief – e.g. believing that someone is trying to kill them and to prevent this they take action against the person.	While this may be true in a small number of cases, the vast majority of people with delusional ideas do not act on them.
Command auditory hallucinations (i.e. those that contain instructions to behave in a particular way) are an indicator of risk, though consistent evidence for a simple relationship is lacking.	Zisook *et al* (1995) found that people with command hallucinations were no more violent than matched controls.

One of the few learning disability studies that have been conducted found that those with a diagnosis of schizophrenia were more likely to commit a violent offence than offenders with intellectual disabilities and mood disorders. Once treated, those with a diagnosis of schizophrenia had lower re-offending rates compared to those without (Smith *et al*, 2008).

People with learning disabilities are reported to suffer from increased rates of minor depressive symptoms, although there is no established relationship between persistent mood disorders and offending behaviour. However, irritability, which can be a feature of depressive illness, might lead to aggressive or anti-social behaviour, while other mood disorders such as mania – where people may behave in a grandiose, irritable or disinhibited way – might lead to public order offences. However, if it is the case that mental illness does increase risk of offending, it follows that treatment will decrease risk of offending. What we have seen more recently is an increase of diagnoses such as personality disorder (PD) and attention deficit and hyperactivity disorder (ADHD) linked to offending populations.

It is estimated that in high secure settings, more than half the population have a diagnosis of learning disability, and at least a quarter in medium and low secure services (Lindsay *et al*, 2006) with LD are characterised by high rates of reoffending (Alexander *et al*, 2006). ADHD is linked with behavioural problems, poor concentration and poor impulse control, which are important risk considerations for future offending behaviour, with up to 20-25% of prisoners diagnosed with ADHD (Young *et al*, 2018).

Another factor often associated with offending and mental health is substance misuse. It was widely believed that people with learning disability had a lower prevalence of substance misuse, however recent figures in offending populations suggest that this is not the case. People using substances are more likely to suffer with mental illness and those with learning disability may be more at risk of adverse effects from substance use given the nature of developmental delay. It is estimated that 90% of the cost of drugs to society is linked to offending (UKDPC, 2008).

Supporting offenders with a learning disability in the CJS

The Criminal Justice System

There are a number of considerations to protect the rights of people with learning disability in the CJS. There are four main stages within the CJS (see figure 1), and there are a number of things that can be done to support individuals at each stage.

Figure 1: The CJS

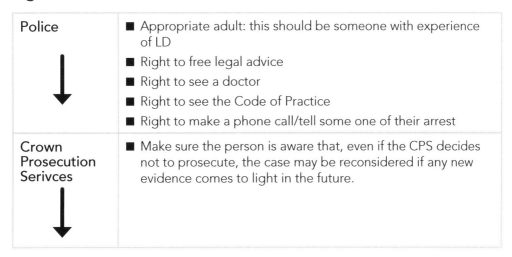

Police	■ Appropriate adult: this should be someone with experience of LD ■ Right to free legal advice ■ Right to see a doctor ■ Right to see the Code of Practice ■ Right to make a phone call/tell some one of their arrest
Crown Prosecution Serivces	■ Make sure the person is aware that, even if the CPS decides not to prosecute, the case may be reconsidered if any new evidence comes to light in the future.

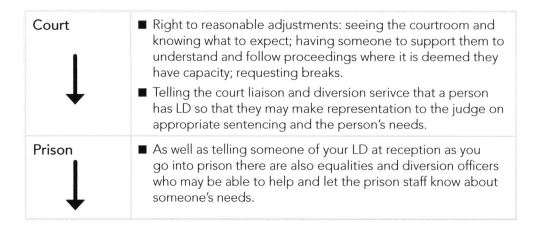

Court	■ Right to reasonable adjustments: seeing the courtroom and knowing what to expect; having someone to support them to understand and follow proceedings where it is deemed they have capacity; requesting breaks.
	■ Telling the court liaison and diversion serivce that a person has LD so that they may make representation to the judge on appropriate sentencing and the person's needs.
Prison	■ As well as telling someone of your LD at reception as you go into prison there are also equalities and diversion officers who may be able to help and let the prison staff know about someone's needs.

Although there are a number of safeguards to support adults with learning disability in the CJS, one of the big issues is poor identification and a lack of screening for this group. Therefore, if you are supporting someone you should encourage them to tell the police they have learning disability as this will entitle them to the support of an appropriate adult.

Identification and support

It is vital that all professionals involved in the CJS are aware of an individual's learning disability. This is so that adjustments can be made to support the person to understand the processes and procedures that they will be subjected to and to support them to understand the nature of any alleged offences they may have committed.

Reasonable adjustments can be made to facilitate access to the CJS, such as Easy Read and accessible information, access to 'relaxed courts' (where the judge dispenses of potentially intimidating gowns and wigs, for example), advocacy and a responsible adult. It may also alert the authorities to any mitigating circumstances surrounding the alleged offence, for example grooming and manipulation by other criminals to exploit the person with a learning disability, which may affect sentencing options.

Police

Looking at our model of the CJS in figure 1, the first stage is the police who will arrest anyone alleged to have committed an offence. While completing their investigation they can hold a person for up to 24 hours. This can be increased for serious crimes or terrorist offences to between 36 or 96 hours, and 14 days, respectively. Under the Police and Criminal Evidence Act (1984), vulnerable persons are not only allowed copies of their rights but also an appropriate adult. An appropriate adult is responsible for protecting (or 'safeguarding') the rights of those deemed vulnerable who are either detained by police or voluntarily interviewed under caution. (See figure 2 for the role of the appropriate adult.)

Figure 2: The role of appropriate adults

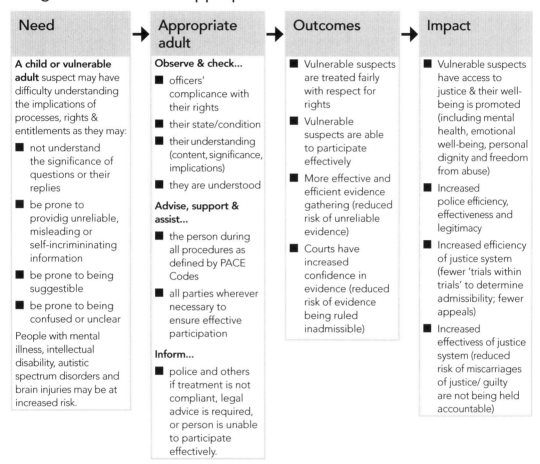

(National Appropriate Adult Network, 2016)

The police may decide, following assessment, to take no further action and the case will be closed or they might administer a caution. A police caution can be controversial, particularly if the person does not fully understand the consequences of admitting guilt. If further action is required, the police can charge the individual and present the case to the Crown Prosecution Service (CPS).

The Crown Prosecution Service

The CPS will decide whether to proceed to a court hearing. To make this decision, the CPS must consider whether it is likely to result in a conviction and whether prosecuting is in the public interest.

Court

When appearing at court, both defendants and witnesses should be able to understand and participate effectively in the court process, as required by Article 6 of the European Convention on Human Rights and by the Human Rights Act (1998) in the UK, and they must have five minimum rights:

- To be informed properly, in a language which he or she understands and in detail, of the nature and cause of the accusation against him.

- To have adequate time and facilities for the preparation of their defence.

- To defend himself in person or through legal assistance of his own choosing or, if he has not sufficient means to pay for legal assistance, to be given it free when the interests of justice so require.

- To examine or to have examined witnesses against him and to obtain the attendance and examination of witnesses on his behalf under the same conditions as witnesses against him.

- To have the free assistance of an interpreter if he cannot understand or speak the language used in court.

Those committed to trial must be able to follow the court proceedings, question evidence, answer questions and instruct counsel.

In court there is the provision of special measures available for vulnerable witnesses to provide evidence. These include the use of screens so they are not intimidated by the defendant, giving evidence via a live television link, clearing the public gallery so that evidence can be given in private, the removal of wigs and gowns in court, and the provision of intermediaries. There is a lack of parity between support for vulnerable witnesses and vulnerable defendants in terms of who is considered vulnerable by the court to require special measures. For example children will always be seen as vulnerable.

The capacity and ability to follow proceedings is required at the Magistrates Court and an assessment may be requested by the court from a mental health professional such as a psychiatrist, whereas issues of fitness to plead are only considered at the Crown Court.

Court disposal: assessment and treatment units

Following a trial, if a defendant with a learning disability is found guilty then the Judge has a range of disposal options. These can include suspended sentences, community service, or a custodial sentence, either in prison or in a secure hospital. Many people with a learning disability will be diverted from the CJS into specialist forensic health services, detained under the Mental Health Act. These hospitals can treat mental illness and rehabilitate offenders through education and treatment programmes. However, following the Winterbourne View scandal and the Transforming Care Agenda, many such beds within learning disability services face closure as more local and community based services are developed. While such beds for the majority of people with a learning disability are not required, and care and support can be provided in the community, those who have been through the CJS and are directed by the courts to secure services for treatment will continue to need them. For more community disposals there needs to be more awareness and expertise in learning disabilities working within the court.

Supporting people to reduce re-offending

There are no medications to stop a person offending. However, for those with a mental illness, medication may decrease symptoms, which in some cases may reduce the risk of further offending. For the majority of learning disability offenders with mental illness it is uncommon to achieve such a straightforward and simple outcome. One exception may be the treatment of ADHD, where the use of stimulant medication may reduce the risk of aggressive or antisocial behaviours in line with psychological treatments. Psychological treatments and psychosocial interventions are delivered individually and in groups. Treatment may be aimed at both co-existing mental illness or be offence-specific, for example sex offences, arson and violent offences. Many interventions for learning disability offenders currently available are based on cognitive behavioural approaches (see Courtney and Rose, 2004; Keeling *et al*, 2008; Sex Offender Treatment Services Collaborative, 2010) whether in the community or hospital. These programmes are often delivered by specialist psychiatrists, psychologists, nurses and occupational therapists working with the individual.

Risk

Comprehensive and holistic risk assessments should be undertaken with the person with a learning disability who has offended and all those involved in their lives. This enables proactive and reactive management plans to be agreed and implemented to reduce the risk of re-offending and maintain public safety while providing the least restrictive conditions for the individual. Such programmes are undertaken after extensive assessment and they should be frequently reviewed to ensure that they are working. Care and support staff are often pivotal in carrying out any plans and feeding back about experiences to the wider team, and consistency, good observation and documentation is therefore important.

Conclusion

Although the evidence for a link between crime and low IQ is robust, there is still doubt about how this applies to people with learning disabilities. While there is a greater prevalence of mental illness in people with learning disabilities, the reported association between mental disorder and offending varies greatly between studies. Offenders with learning disabilities as a clinical population present with significant co-morbidity of mental and physical health and neuro-developmental problems, cognitive and social impairment, lower socio-economic status, poorer housing and issues such as substance abuse, which together highlight the difficulty in determining the link between learning disabilities and offending, and the role each individual factor plays in increasing the likelihood of offending.

Key learning points

- Although crime is linked to intelligence there is no evidence to suggest people with learning disabilities are more likely to commit offences than anyone else.

- As in the general population, the characteristics that predict crime are largely similar, such as poverty and substance use.

- Within the CJS there are a number of safeguards in place, including appropriate adults in police stations, intermediaries and special measures that can be taken, and reasonable adjustments that can be made. However, these can be different for witnesses and defendants.

References

Alexander RT, Crouch K, Halstead S & Pichaud J (2006) Long-term outcome from a medium secure service for people with intellectual disability. *Journal of Intellectual Disability Research* **50** (4) 305–315.

Courtney J & Rose J (2004) The effectiveness of treatment for male sex offenders with learning disabilities: a review of the literature. *Journal of sexual aggression* **10** (2) pp215–236.

McCarthy J, Chaplin E, Underwood L, Forrester A, Hayward H, Sabet J, Young S, Asherson P, Mills R & Murphy D (2016) Characteristics of prisoners with neurodevelopmental disorders and difficulties. *Journal of Intellectual Disability Research* **60** (3) pp201–206.

Rose J, Rose D, Hawkins C & Anderson C (2012) A sex offender treatment group for men with intellectual disabilities in a community setting. *The British Journal of Forensic Practice* **14** (1) pp21–28.

Smith H, White T & Walker P (2008) Offending in the learning disabled population: a retrospective audit of Tayside learning disability service court reports. *Medicine, Science and the Law* **48** (1) 31–36.

UK Drug Policy Commission (2008) *Reducing Drug Use, Reducing Reoffending*. London: UKDPC.

Young S, González RA, Mullens H, Mutch L, Malet-Lambert I & Gudjonsson GH (2018) Neurodevelopmental disorders in prison inmates: comorbidity and combined associations with psychiatric symptoms and behavioural disturbance. *Psychiatry research* **261** pp109–115.

Zisook S, Byrd D, Kuck J & Jeste DV (1995) Command hallucinations in outpatients with schizophrenia. *Journal of Clinical Psychiatry* **56** 462–465.

Further resources and other titles from Pavilion Publishing

Challenging Behaviour and People with Intellectual Disabilities: A handbook (2nd edition)

By Peter Baker and Tony Osgood

Successful Health Screening Through Desensitisation for People with Learning Disabilities

A learning resource pack for healthcare professionals

By Lisa Harrington and Sarah Walker

Intellectual Disabilities and Personality Disorder

An integrated approach to support

By Dr Zillah Webb

The Mental Capacity Act and People with Learning Disabilities

A training pack to develop good practice in assessing capacity and making best interests decisions

By Theresa Joyce and Steve Hardy

Mental Health in Intellectual Disabilities (5th edition)

A resource for support staff and managers in learning disability services

Edited by Dr Colin Hemmings

Person-centred Active Support (2nd edition)

A training resource and self-study guide to enable participation, independence and choice for adults and children with developmental disabilities

By Professor Julie Beadle-Brown, Bev Murphy and Dr Jill Bradshaw

Personal Development, Relationships and Staying Safe

This training resource gives frontline staff the skills and knowledge to support safe personal relationships for people with complex or high support needs

By Marie Walsh and Geraldine Cregg

Sex and the 3 Rs: Rights, Risks and Responsibilities (4th edition)

A sex education resource for working with people with learning disabilities

By Dr Michelle McCarthy and David Thompson

Sexuality and Learning Disabilities (2nd edition)

Edited by Claire Bates

Sex, Personal Relationships and the Law for Adults with Learning Disabilities

A guide to decision making in England and Wales, including the Mental Capacity Act (2005) and the Sexual Offences Act (2003)

By David Thompson

Supporting Derek

A practice development guide to support staff working with people who have a learning difficulty and dementia

By Karen Watchmen, Diana Kerr and Dr Heather Wilkinson

Successful Health Screening Through Desensitisation for People with Learning Disabilities

A training and resource pack for healthcare professionals

By Lisa Harrington and Sarah Walker

Supporting the Physical Health Needs of People with Learning Disabilities

A handbook for professionals, support staff and families

By Steve Hardy, Eddie Chaplin and Peter Woodward